ROBERT MURRAY McCHEYNE

Alexander Smellie (1857-1923) was born in Stranraer, Scotland. After his theological studies, he returned there to pastor an Original Secession Church. He also ministered in Thurso (1894-1900) and in Carluke (1900-1923). Smellie looked forward to the reunion of the evangelical Presbyterian denominations in Scotland and had cordial relations with Christians in other churches. As a writer, he is best-known for his *Men of the Covenant* which has been translated into several languages.

ROBERT MURRAY McCHEYNE

ALEXANDER SMELLIE

#6

CHRISTIAN FOCUS PUBLICATIONS

The Publishers have added to Alexander Smellie's *Robert Murray McCheyne*, extracts from the diary of Jessie Thain and an account of the revival in Dundee by Rev. Alexander Cumming. Both Jessie Thain and Alexander Cumming were friends of McCheyne.

© Christian Focus Publications
ISBN 1-85792-184-4

Published in 1995 by
Christian Focus Publications Ltd.
Geanies House, Fearn, Ross-shire,
IV20 1TW, Scotland, Great Britain.

Cover design by Donna Macleod

Printed and bound in Great Britain by
The Guernsey Press Co. Ltd., Guernsey, Channel Islands

Computer setting by Bell Publishing Services,
01730 825776.

Contents

ROBERT MURRAY McCHEYNE

EXTRACTS FROM THE DIARY OF JESSIE THAIN

SOME INCIDENTS CONNECTED WITH THE REVIVAL IN DUNDEE (1839-40)

Preface

This little book may be said to have a double parentage. The first suggestion of it came from Dr. F. B. Meyer and those associated with him in the Council of the English Free Churches. They desired to include, in their series of Leaders of Revival, a volume which should treat McCheyne and William Burns, and of that work of grace in Scotland with which these shining names are unbreakably linked; and they were good enough to ask me to write the volume.

But then, some months afterwards, in a curious and quite unexpected way, there was sent to me from Mr. James Macdonald, W.S., of Edinburgh, an altogether priceless box of McCheyne manuscripts – letters to and from his family and friends, notebooks, sermons, and documents of different kinds.[1] Mr. Macdonald knew nothing of Dr. Meyer's previous invitation; and it seemed strange that I should have this twofold call to write about Robert Murray McCheyne.

But now I had to expand somewhat the scope of the book. If I were to take advantage of the treasure-trove of manuscripts put at my disposal, it became evident that I must try to portray McCheyne not only as a leader of revival but in

---

1. The box, with its contents, Mr Macdonald proposes to give to the Jewish Committee of the United Free Church of Scotland, to be preserved in the Library of the New College, Edinburgh. It was bought by him from Mr William Scott of Thornhill, one of the few surviving relatives of The McCheynes. A younger brother of Adam McCheyne, Robert's father, was William, who emigrated to America and died there. He had a son, James; and James's daughter was Jean McCheyne, who married Mr Scott. She, too, died a few years ago.

more personal aspects of his character – as a son, a brother, a friend, and a minister of the Gospel of Christ. I fear that this alteration of plan may have been disappointing to the office-bearers of the Free Church Council, although they have shown themselves exceedingly magnanimous and patient throughout. Yet surely it would have been a pity not to utilize the new material to which I had been given access.

I am the debtor also of Miss Marjory Bonar, who has helped me very kindly and effectively, allowing me to avail myself of her father's memoranda and marginalia, and herself clearing away more than one difficulty.

It is, of course, impossible, even with such conspicuous assistance as I have had, to add much to what is recorded in the *Memoir and Remains*. Once for all, Dr. Andrew Bonar has limned the features of his friend; and he who comes after Dr. Bonar can only be, like the Arab physician, 'a picker-up of learning's crumbs'. But I shall be glad if I succeed in sending some new readers to a biography which is, and will always be, a possession of the heart; and, for the rest, if, in the pages that follow, I have caught one or two human and homely glimpses of a white-robed saint. It has been a wonderful and sacred privilege to be permitted, in his centenary year, to lay a stone of remembrance on Robert McCheyne's cairn.

February, 1913.

To the Glory of God,
and in memory of
ROBERT MURRAY McCHEYNE

CHAPTER 1

Winter Passeth After The Long Delay

Between the Scotland of the seventeenth century and its successor of the eighteenth the contrasts are many and notable. 'Mountains divide them, and the waste of seas.' Outwardly, the changes of the new era were entirely for the better. Political stability and rest were substituted for turmoil and war. Social progress went forward by leaps and bounds. The prosperity and the wealth of the country were vastly increased. But religion did not gain ground; it waned and receded. There was a note of culture and elegance in its expression which had not been there formerly; it had become careful of the proprieties; it dressed itself in velvets and satins instead of in the homespun with which the fathers had been content. But the fire and the fervour had left its heart. It was icily regular. A frost had fallen upon it; and it was no longer the burning and blazing passion which went singing into the fight at Drumclog, or up the scaffold-steps at the Mercat Cross and the Gallow-Lee.

Perhaps we may acquaint ourselves best with this difference of atmosphere, if we peep into one or two books which are famous in Scottish literature.

This, for example, is Robert Wodrow's *Analecta*. It describes the decadence in its beginnings. It is the voluminous and garrulous and always interesting diary in which the minister of Eastwood has set down, from March 1701 to December 1731, 'what he happened to hear from good hands and well-attested'. Wodrow is himself evangelical, and does not lose sight of 'the great red light of Calvary'. But he is far from being an extremist in his evangelism.

For instance, when the Assembly of 1720 has condemned *The Marrow of Modern Divinity*, the little English treatise which Hog of Carnock and Boston of Ettrick had introduced to readers north of the Tweed, whose chapters ring forth in its fullness and its freeness the music of the gospel, and when the Assembly of 1722 has rebuked the twelve Marrowmen at its bar, Wodrow, because he is a staunch upholder of the conclusions and decisions of the authorities of the Church, is in perfect sympathy with the Assembly. The man of order and prudence is generally a trifle suspicious of the man who scorns the consequence, and follows his soul wherever it may lead.

Yet this quiet and sober Churchman was filled with concern as he surveyed the religious conditions of his time. The young men of Glasgow, he writes, did not have the training in Christian faith and conduct to which their predecessors had been accustomed; and, going abroad in the pursuit of trade, they came back with the laxer habits of other lands. At the University the students, and those in the Divinity classes not least, were disclosing a tendency to freedom of thought; and the statement by the Professors of Trinitarian doctrine excited appearances of dissent and even of derision. In the city where, a few winters previously, there had been seventy-two regular meetings for prayer, Wodrow knew now of only five; while clubs for debating on miscellaneous and often irreverent questions were coming into vogue.

When the watchful minister marked such ominous symptoms, the fear stole into his breast that a desolating stroke must be impending over the West Country, once the peculiar home of the saints, but now 'ensnared, assaulted, overcome, led bound'.

With the teaching of numbers of his fellow-clergymen he was as profoundly dissatisfied. In these early decades of the eighteenth century Scotland witnessed the birth of what, somewhat later, was to be designated Moderatism. The younger preachers no longer spoke, in the dialect of their forebears, about sin and salvation, atonement and conversion, faith and repentance; the words, and the truths behind the words, were regarded as hopelessly antiquated, if not as quite obsolete. The pulpit was giving itself, instead, to the discussion of the moralities of daily conduct, the ethics of Scripture, the decencies of good behaviour. But to Wodrow these prelections were pithless, nerveless, toothless; and he did not love them.

On a Sacramental Monday, in Glasgow, he hearkened to a discourse from Mr Wallace of Moffat, on the text, *Faith without works is dead*. It was 'in the new haranguing method', and it pleased 'some of the young volage sparks who set up now mightily for criticks'. For a full half-hour the speaker insisted on the necessity of inquiry in religion, and so left only a quarter of an hour in which to give a cold account of faith as an assent and crediting of the truth; and then he closed with a fling at all imposed forms of orthodoxy.

Again, in the Assembly of 1730, the minister of Eastwood heard, from the lips of Mr Telfer of Hawick, 'one of the wildest out-of-the-way sermons'. It was a satire on the old days, to which Robert Wodrow looked back wistfully. It had many a jeer at those who mourned the declensions of the present. It commended the industry and virtue, the improvements in science, the advances in commerce and comfort, which the

preacher discovered among his contemporaries. And so, 'with
an inference or two of the duty of praise and thankfulness',
the laughing philosopher concluded. One listener at least was
ill at ease about 'such confident impudence'. The optimist
had gone to Solomon for his text; and the softest thing Mr
Wodrow could say of him was contained in another word of
Solomon, *Thou hast not wisely considered this*. His own mind
was made up. He could not abide these 'loose, general, inco-
herent' essays in the rudiments of morals, 'with some turns
out of Shaftsburry, the *Tatlers* and *Spectators*, and such odd
common-places for ministers'. He was nurtured himself on
stronger meat. And he was certain that it would be a sad day
for the Scottish Kirk when she preferred pointless platitudes
to the humbling and healing and bracing and regenerating
verities of the gospel of Christ.

Such were 'the check, the change, the fall' in their earlier
manifestations. To ascertain how rapidly and how ruinously
they progressed we may leave Robert Wodrow for Alexander Carlyle, whose imposing presence won for him the so-
briquet of 'Jupiter' Carlyle: 'he was,' says Sir Walter Scott,
'the grandest demigod I ever saw.' For fifty-seven summers
and winters from his ordination in 1748 until his death in
1805, he was minister of the parish of Inveresk. Side by side
with Principal William Robertson he led the Moderates in
the Church of Scotland; and his *Autobiography*, which John
Hill Burton published in 1860, tells us what sort of leader he
was. Though he did not sit down to write it till the day he
entered his seventy-ninth year, few books are so forceful and
racy, so alert and keen-eyed; but its vitality is that of a capable man of the world, and no breath of spirituality stirs in its
pages.

We are introduced to Dukes and Lords of Session and

great ladies; for, as his parishioners hinted, and as he was himself ready to confess, Alexander Carlyle was 'partial to the company of his superiors'. We meet and talk with prominent men of letters – John Home of *Douglas* fame and Tobias Smollett, Adam Smith and David Hume. We are taken to see Garrick, both in his residence at Hampton and on the stage in Drury Lane; 'of the many exertions I and my friends have made for the credit and interest of the clergy of the Church of Scotland', our annalist boasts in a characteristic passage, 'there was none more meritorious and of better effects than this', that, in spite of protests and libels from his Presbytery, he set the fashion of ministerial playgoing. We gain admission to the various social clubs which the parson of Inveresk patronised or helped to found – the Select Society, the Poker Club, the Tuesday Club, the Diversorium; like the market-place of Yarmouth, they were 'remarkably well-provided with every kind of vivres for the pot and the spit', and 'the wine is excellent and flows freely': first and last, Jupiter Carlyle plumed himself not only on his 'Parnassian correspondence' but on his 'Olympian conviviality'.

Or, again, we find him initiating Principal Robertson and Dr. Hugh Blair into the mysteries of backgammon and whist, though both of his pupils have passed their sixtieth birthday; he was an accomplished tutor, for, in the manses of the neighbourhood, he had 'set the first example of playing at cards at home with unlocked doors, and so had relieved the clergy from ridicule on that side': 'Robertson did very well, Blair never shone'; but now at least they need not any more be 'very unhappy when in friends' houses in the country in rainy weather'.

It is all clever and engrossing after its own manner and in its own accent; but the accent is not that of the 'country afar beyond the stars', nor the manner that in which 'true Aarons are drest'. The truth is that the *Autobiography* is frankly and unashamedly secular, when it is not altogether pagan. And we are not surprised that Carlyle's theology was broad and latitudinarian. At the Divinity Hall in Edinburgh, in the winter of 1741-42, he had prescribed to him as a theme for discourse, *De Fide Salvifica*. He wrote his thesis, and delivered it; but it was 'a very improper subject for so young a student'. One fears that to the end Dr Carlyle kept far away in his preaching from the doctrine of Saving Faith.

Some time in 1753, David Hume heard him in Athelstaneford Church, on a Sabbath when he was doing duty for John Home. Afterwards, when they met before dinner, 'What did you mean,' the philosopher queried, 'by treating John's congregation today with one of Cicero's academics? I did not think,' he added, 'that such heathen morality would have passed in East Lothian.' Carlyle, in fact, makes no attempt to hide his distaste for all that is mystical and supernatural in religion. 'There arose such murmuring in the parish against me,' he acknowledges in one of his outspoken paragraphs, 'together with many doubts about my having the grace of God – an occult quality which the people cannot define'; and we detect the sting and sneer in those last words. For the men of the opposite party in the Church he had little patience and abundant contempt. He nicknamed them 'the Highflyers', and made fun of them whenever he could. Primrose of Crichton was 'a shallow pedant', puffed up by the flattery of his brethren to think himself an eminent scholar: 'he had a fluent elocution in the dialect of Morayshire, embellished with English of his own invention; but with all this he had no common sense'. Smith of Cranston was 'a sly northern'; Watson of Newbattle, 'a dark inquisi-

tor', all the more dangerous because he was 'of some parts';
Walker of Temple, 'a rank enthusiast, with nothing but heat
without light'. It was the light that Carlyle himself prized,
the *Aufklärung*, the Illuminism; for the enthusiasm and the
heat he never pretended to cherish any affection.

Probably the *Autobiography* shows us Moderatism in its
most arid and unprofitable phase; there were men on the same
side in the General Assembly who had felt the touch of the
Highest. And, confronting them, fighting a long and dour
campaign against them, stood the Evangelicals, who, as the
century ran on towards its close, gained gradually and surely
in influence. Moreover, Scotland had sons and daughters
outside the bounds of the Established Church, who lived near
Christ, and therefore near the hearth-fire; Cameronians, who
had never accepted the Revolution Settlement; Seceders, of
the family of Ebenezer and Ralph Erskine, or of the other
family of Thomas Gillespie; later still, the worshippers in
those Independent chapels which Robert and James Haldane
founded in many parts of the country. The leaven of grace
was working, and the hour was at hand when the issues of its
processes would be revealed more plainly. God and His saints
held fellowship when things looked driest and deadest.

In the opening sentences of another delectable book, the
Memorials of his Time, Henry Cockburn, who was born in
October 1779, describes one of these saints. 'My mother,'
he writes, 'was the best woman I have ever known. If I were
to survive her for a thousand years, I should still have a deep
and grateful recollection of her kindness, her piety, her devotion to her family, and her earnest, gentle, and Christian
anxiety for their happiness in this life and in the life to come.'
Lord Cockburn is certain, too, that there was much true religion in that older generation which he recalls with such viv-

idness and charm; though 'my opinion is,' he avowed in 1830, 'that the balance is in favour of the present time.'

In his final pages he introduces us to the man who, in the shaping and refining hand of God, did more than any other to usher in the better era. Thomas Chalmers, he says, 'is awkward, and has a low, husky voice, a gutteral articulation, a whitish eye, and a large dingy countenance.' In point of mere feature, indeed, it would not be difficult to think him ugly. But he was saved from this, and made interesting and lovable, by singular modesty and simplicity of manner, a strong expression of calm thought and benevolence, a forehead so broad that it seemed to proclaim itself the seat of a great intellect, and a love of humour and drollery. And such a consummate orator he was, in spite of his bad figure, voice, gesture, and look, and the uncouthness of his Doric accent.

Often Cockburn had 'hung upon his words with a beating heart and a tearful eye'. The magic lay in the concentrated intensity which agitated every fibre of the man, and kindled his speech as if with living fire. 'He no sooner approaches the edge of his high region, than his animation converts his external defects into positive advantages by showing the intellectual power that overcomes them; and, when he has got us at last within the flames of his enthusiasm, Jeffrey's description that he "buried his adversaries under the fragments of burning mountains" is the only image that suggests an idea of his eloquent imagination and terrible energy'. Best of all, he appeared to Henry Cockburn to be utterly unspoiled by applause.

The Memoirs of Thomas Chalmers, which his son-in-law, Dr. William Hanna, has written, is the last of these books with which we ought to hold converse, if we wish to see how, a hundred years back, the life of God was faring in the soul of Scotland. It is a big undertaking to read Dr. Hanna's four massive volumes – too big for him whose mental food is the sevenpenny novel and the magazine article and the evening newspaper; but the lovers of that literature which educates and inspires can never get too much of it, and we have it here at its best. It accelerates our sluggishness, it instils a medicinal euphrasy and rue into our dull vision, it sweetens our petulant and distrustful temper, and it builds us into finer and more Christlike men and women, to walk and talk with Dr. Chalmers in the leisurely fashion which this satisfying biography permits us to do; and when we have arrived at its conclusion, we would not have it abridged by a single page.

It has many a time been said that the German Reformation was wrought out in the first instance, and in miniature, within the heart and history of Martin Luther himself; and the reformation which Thomas Chalmers so emphatically achieved for his native land was the outcome of the remarkable change which made him, in his own thoughts and words and ways, a new creation in Christ Jesus. The third chapter of the *Memoirs* describes his ordination to his Fifeshire parish of Kilmany, in the Maytime of 1803; but we have to journey on to the eighth chapter, and the winter of 1811, before the preacher has any gospel to proclaim. Through the intervening years he was more interested in mathematics than in the New Testament, and in his lectures to the students of St Andrews on chemistry and geology than in the spiritual welfare of his people.

'The author of this pamphlet,' he wrote in self-defence, 'can assert, from what to him is the highest of all authority, the authority of his own experience, that, after the satisfactory discharge of his parish duties, a minister may enjoy five days in the week of uninterrupted leisure for the prosecution of any science in which his taste may dispose him to engage.' Years afterwards, in what was 'perhaps the most imposing single passage in his life', in a debate on Pluralities in the Assembly of 1825, he recanted the words and confessed his error amid the deathlike stillness of the House. 'I have no reserve in saying that the sentiment was wrong, and that, in the utterance of it, I penned what was most outrageously wrong. Strangely blinded that I was! What, sir, is the object of mathematical science? Magnitude, and the proportions of magnitude. But then, sir, I had forgotten two magnitudes. I thought not of the littleness of time; I recklessly thought not of the greatness of eternity.'

What awakened him to the greatness of eternity was his perusal of Wilberforce's *Practical View of Christianity*. It taught him that, on the principle of *Do this and live*, no peace, and no true and worthy obedience, could ever be attained. It turned him right round, to an unquestioning adoption of the contrary principle, *Believe in the Lord Jesus Christ, and thou shalt be saved*. 'I sicken at all my own imperfect preparations,' he confessed; 'I take one decisive and immediate step, and resign my all to the sufficiency of my Saviour.' He boasted, he said more than once, 'in the plenitude of the great Atonement'.

From that birth-hour momentous consequences flowed. Kilmany first felt the thrill. Chalmers had another message in the pulpit now, and another success among his parishioners. He had inculcated the need of moral improvement, with that eager and fervid eloquence which was natural to him. He had expatiated on the meanness of dishonesty, on the villainy of falsehood, on the despicable arts of calumny. It had not occurred to him that, although he had effected the ethical revival which he desired, the hearts of his auditors would have continued as destitute of the essence of religion as ever. But even the honour, the truth, and the integrity, for which he had pleaded with such perseverance, were not secured. 'It was not till reconciliation to God became the distinct and the prominent object of my exertions; it was not till the free offer of forgiveness by the blood of Christ was urged upon their acceptance, and the Holy Spirit was set before them as the unceasing object of their dependence and their prayers; that I ever heard of any of those subordinate reforms which I made the earnest and the zealous, but, I am afraid, the ultimate, object of my ministrations.'

So the Fifeshire village was changed into a garden, full of shelter and of fountains. And that was but the commencement. In Glasgow, in Edinburgh, throughout all Scotland, Chalmers was soon to be the harbinger of an acceptable year of the Lord. The time of famine was giving place at last to the time of fruit. The Illuminism was being transfigured into heat and glow.

Now, it was into this new stir of spiritual life that Robert McCheyne was born; and in the vital air he found his proper climate and home. He was, in truth, to make the air yet more quickening and ethereal. For, if he had not the largeness and the splendour of Chalmers, he burned out for God with a still intenser flame.

CHAPTER 2

The Training of a Good Husbandman

Three agencies shaped Robert Murray McCheyne into the manner of man he became. There were the wholesome influences of his early home. There was the education of school and college. Most decisive of all, there was the grace of God.

He was born at 14 Dublin Street, Edinburgh, on the 21st of May, 1813, the youngest child in a family of five. One of his brothers, David Thomas, was between eight and nine years his senior.

Next came the sister, Eliza Mary, who entered so largely into Robert's biography, living under his roof and caring for him during the swift and strenuous days of the ministry in Dundee. 'How art thou thyself, my own Deaconess and help-meet of thy poor brother?' he asked her in a letter sent from the wilds of Galicia; and had he known them, he might have used about her Christina Rossetti's words, that 'There is no friend like a sister in calm or stormy weather'. Eliza Mary McCheyne lived to be a white-haired woman of eighty-two, carrying in her heart through all her later history a great store of gracious and touching memories.

Another brother followed, William Oswald Hunter. His life, also, though it was shadowed by frequent illnesses and depressions, was a very long one; for he survived his sister by four years and a half, and died in his native city in the October of 1892.

Then there was a little girl, Isabella, born in the autumn of 1811, whom Robert never saw in this lower world; she passed from the earthly home when she was nine months old: like 'pretty Johnny' Lightmaker, Archbishop Leighton's nephew, she 'was gone an hour or two sooner to bed, as children use to do – and we are undressing to follow'.

These were the young people, and we shall meet some of them again. But first we must look into the faces of the parents, and try to estimate their characters. Fathers and mothers mean so much to the children, and dower them with such inheritances of good or ill.

Adam McCheyne had come as a boy from the Dumfriesshire village of Thornhill to Edinburgh. He was a lawyer – not an advocate practising at the Bar in the Parliament House, but a Writer to the Signet: one of that 'ancient society of solicitors in Scotland, who formerly had the exclusive right to prepare all summonses and other writs pertaining to the Supreme Court of Justice', and who still retain the premier position among the various societies of law agents.

He was a man of social importance, who had more than an average share of the world's wealth and goods. That his means were considerable is proved by the homes in which he lived. When Robert was six, the Dublin Street house was forsaken for a residence in Queen Street – 'dear old 56', as its occupier calls it fondly; and Queen Street, with its roomy and dignified mansions, its gardens and leafy trees, and its glorious prospects of the Firth of Forth and the shores of Fife, is not one of those thoroughfares where poor men stay.

Through sixteen years, all the time of the boy's schooling and of his attendance at the University, this was the home of the family. It would never have been left, if the landlord had not been 'a bit of a Nabal who refused to do what was required in the way of repairs'; but when, in 1835, the good-byes were spoken, Mr. McCheyne migrated to a yet more commodious house, though now there were no sea-glimpses nor green gardens, at 20 Hill Street; and it is to 20 Hill Street, that the letters of the probationer and the minister of St Peter's are addressed.

One gathers an impression of Adam McCheyne as a capable, shrewd, trusted, and trustworthy man of business, in whose advice his clients would confide with implicit faith: a man, moreover, whose opinions on politics and public affairs were clear-cut and strong. He was frankly Tory; there would have been no Reform Act if he had had his way; Sir Robert Peel was the statesman to whom he gave loyal allegiance. 'Have you any vermin called Whigs and Radicals or Radical-Whigs in Hindustan?' he writes to his son William; 'if you have, I pray you to keep clear of them; they are very venomous creatures.'

He was master in his own house; and 'it was no part of my character,' he acknowledges, 'to spare the rod.' The children here were expected to reverence their parents. But he was as approachable as he was firm. We read the letters which his boys wrote to him, and they are absolutely unconstrained and free; they acquaint him with every secret; they laugh and joke and have no fear; he is more than father – he is intimate and friend. His birthday fell on the 27th of January; and first it was David, and then it was Robert, who, with filial piety, composed in his honour year by year a Birthday Ode.

> Time with us has left no traces
>   Of his power to damp our mirth;
> Still we have the same gay faces
>   Smiling round our happy hearth –

David sang on one of these January mornings; and nine years later, when 'the first-born' was 'the first-dead' too, Robert, away in Torwood, took up the strain:

> Where the Carron's flooded water
>   Dashes on its wintry way,
> There thy youngest son and daughter
>   Bless thee on thy natal day.

He was a good man, as well as a righteous, who could call forth such verses as these.

Before her marriage in 1802, Robert McCheyne's mother had been Lockhart Murray Dickson, the youngest daughter of David Dickson, proprietor of Nether Locharwood, in the parish of Ruthwell and the county of Dumfries. The lines of her portrait are less distinct than those of her lawyer husband. But we feel ourselves in the presence of a nature more buoyant, more light-hearted, at times more gay than that of the vigorous Writer to the Signet.

'Robert was from infancy blessed with a sweet, docile, and affectionate temper,' his father wrote of him a month after he had gone; and the enviable adjectives were the mother's legacy to the child. She was womanly in this, that it was her joy to communicate to the young people, when they were absent from her side, all the items of intelligence in which they would be interested; and her son commends her letters as better than any newspaper. Many floods could not drown the love that pulsed within her for her children. 'O, write, write!' she pleads, in a hungry postscript, with the son who was far off in India; and on the back of a sheet penned by the saint who quitted her so soon for the sight of the face of Christ in the New Jerusalem – a sheet which has been lent for a little to a friend – there is a request full of pathos. 'You will please return this to me. I like to keep *all* my dear Robert's letters.'

Father and mother were accustomed to think on those things which are true and honourable and just and pure and lovely; and both by speech and by example they encouraged their children to do the same. But one imagines that the religion of the home became profounder, more Christ-centred and Christ-controlled, as time ran on. We know that Adam McCheyne and his wife were, for years, members of one or another of the Edinburgh Churches in which Moderatism was in the ascendant; and the son often begs them to do what he had himself done before he left home, when he forsook Dr. Muir for John Bruce, in the New North – to seek out a ministry whose tone was definitely and consistently evangelical. Then we cannot but remark that consuming earnestness with which, in almost every letter he writes, he entreats both parents to dig deep and to lay well the foundations of their faith; though this, of course, was Robert McCheyne's habitual dialect after he had discovered that there are, in Rutherfurd's phrase, 'a hoard, a hidden treasure, and a gold mine in Christ you never yet saw'.

Probably stress need not be laid on the measured and sober enjoyments of the household; for Henry Cockburn tells us that these were commoner among Christian people in the teens and twenties of the century than they were in the thirties. But, altogether, the feeling is hardly to be avoided that, in the revolution of the seasons, parents no less than children were drawn much nearer to Him who is the Centre of rest. Trial and bereavement yielded their peaceable fruits. And by and by the passion of their youngest son for Jesus and eternity affected those dearest to him as well as the multitude outside. When, in 1835, Adam McCheyne wrote to that boy of his who was a doctor in Nasirabad, this was his chief anxiety for the lad exposed to the temptations of the foreign land: 'Above all, may He lead and guide you to Himself, and then you will never want a Friend that sticketh closer than a brother'. Mayhap, these mighty transports had moved and thrilled him before; but they had not always been so frankly expressed.[1]

Robert McCheyne did not, like John Stuart Mill, begin to learn Greek at three; but at four, when he was recovering from measles or scarlet fever, his father taught him the Greek alphabet, and he was able to form the letters on his slate. A year later, he was sent to his first school, that of Mr. George Knight. In it he made good progress; and when, a few sessions afterwards, he left the highest class, he carried away the second prize. He was distinguished, in those early days, for his skill in recitation; he had a quick and correct ear and a melodious voice.

His parents attended the Tron Church at the time; and, because the distance from their house in the New Town was too great for the younger children, Eliza, William, and Robert used to remain, in company with others of their own age, in the pews of the church during the interval that divided the morning and afternoon services. In accordance with salutary custom, the boys and girls were catechised by their elders; and there were those who in subsequent years recollected Robert's clear and pleasant articulation, as he repeated his Psalms or the answers of the Westminster Assembly's Catechism. 'The child's voice,' to quote a word of Robert

---

1. McCheyne's father and mother lie buried in St Cuthbert's churchyard, Edinburgh. He died on the 24th of February 1854, aged seventy-four years; she followed him in less than three months, dying on the 15th of May.

Barbour's, 'was like a sound from a better life and a better land, so simple and pure.'

From Mr. Knight the boy went, in October 1821, to the High School – not, indeed, to that beautiful Athenian temple which nestled under the Calton Hill, but to the older building in Infirmary Street; and there, through the four junior classes, Mr. George Irvine was his teacher. In his thirteenth year he reached the Rector's classes, the fifth and the sixth. Dr. Aglionby Ross Carson, rector from 1820 to 1845, was one of the famous headmasters of a famous school; and, under his guidance, McCheyne found a new world of enchantment disclosed to him in the literature of Greece and Rome. A scrapbook survives into which he has copied, in boyish handwriting, some of the exercises done for the headmaster. Here is his first attempt at poetical composition, read at one of the public exhibitions of the school – a blank-verse translation of part of the Second Georgic. Here, too, is his first original poem: a lyric, in true Byronic vein, commiserating the degenerate sons of 'those who won the bloody field of Marathon'; adjuring Greece to 'dare to be free – These fetters ne'er were forged for thee'; and promising her the succour in her distresses of valorous Scotsmen:

> Behold, from Freedom's distant land
> A Cochrane comes with aidful brand.

Here are his earliest Latin verses, hexameters and pentameters and alcaics – expansions of some Virgilian or Horatian or Homeric sentiment, youthful odes *In Lucem* or *Ad Edinam*, or the description of a skirmish of cavalry, or a rendering of *The Battle of Linden*. And here are the lines recited on the closing day, August 6, 1827, when school was left for 'the rugged paths of life'. They recall the books which his comrades and he have read together and the joys they have shared in common. They celebrate the learning and goodness of their Rector:

> Thou, too, Farewell,
> Who hast Antiquity's delightful stores
> To us unlocked! Instructor, Friend, Farewell!

In the *Reminiscences of a Boyhood in the Early Part of the Century*, which Canon Bell of Cheltenham published in 1889, we get a glimpse through the eyes of a companion, of Robert McCheyne in his High School days. 'My recollections,' says Canon Bell, 'are of a tall slender lad with a sweet pleasant face, bright yet grave, fond of play, and of a blameless life. I remember to this day his tartan trousers, which excited my admiration and my envy.'

Others, too, remembered the unusual and national dress. An anonymous magazine article, which travels back to tread again the ancient track of that Edinburgh school-time, speaks of 'the mediaeval-fashioned tunic of green tartan worn by the poet-laureate of Carson's class', whose 'valedictory address drew tears even from old eyes', and how well it 'set off his handsome figure'. He must have been a boy to gladden the sight and to capture the heart.

In the holidays there were excursions for the young people to Dumfriesshire, to Thornhill and Ruthwell, where the warmest welcomes greeted them and where Robert Mc-Cheyne's love of nature had room to reveal itself and grow. His earliest letters home, written in the summer and autumn of 1827, are full of the boy's delight in farmyard and harvest field. On the last day of August, he tells his mother, 'we have much need of David and William, as Auntie is very busy cutting and taking in'. Nearly two months later he is still at Clarencefield Cottage; there was no call to hurry back to Edinburgh in this particular year, for school was ended now, and he was waiting for the University session to begin. So, on October 20th, there is a whole batch of letters: one for his father and mother, bubbling over with playful gaiety; one for Eliza, 'fairest and dearest' – 'All the inhabitants of Clarencefield complain, They have not heard a word from Miss McCheyne'; and one for each of his brothers. That to William concludes with an exhaustive inventory of the farm. 'Auntie has got 7 stacks and 2 barns full; 3 swine, 2 sows, 7 pigs; 8 hens, no cock; 8 ducks, 2 drakes; 1 goose, 1 gander; 1 mare, 1 blood-mare (famous rider), 1 filly; 1 bees' skep; 2 cats; 1 canary; 4 cows, 3 stirks; 2 dogs; 37 cart-load of potatoes; Miss McC, Mrs. D, Miss M D, Joseph, Jenny, David, May, and your affectionate brother, Bob M McCheyne.'

During a previous vacation, in another part of Scotland, he had had something of an adventure. He and the inseparable friend of his boyhood, Malcolm MacGregor, were walking through the wild and picturesque country round Dunkeld. Crossing the hills to Strath Ardle, they were caught in a dense fog, and lost their way. Night came on, and they were forced to make their bed out on the bare ground. At first the absolute stillness of the place frightened them, but the cold and the fear compelled them to lie close to one another; and soon they were sleeping soundly, to be roused at dawn by the sunshine streaming into their faces and by the cries of moorcock and grouse.

Four or five years afterwards, when Malcolm MacGregor, as a young Army officer, was setting out for the other side of the world, his comrade recalled their experience:

Wilt thou ever forget how the thick shades descended,
    And wrapped the wild mountains of Atholl in night;
How horror and terror and wonder were blended,
    When gloomy Loch Oshney[2] invaded our sight?

And O, when we couched 'mong the dark waving heather,
    With mists of the mountain to curtain our head,
How with bosom to bosom we slumbered together,
    Till night with its darkness and dangers had fled?

At the University, first in the classes of the Arts faculty, and then in those of Divinity, McCheyne spent nearly eight years, entering in the winter of 1827, and leaving in the spring of 1835. He was a good student, though not a brilliant one. 'His proficiency was above mediocrity,' his father writes with modest praise; 'and he gained several prizes, though I cannot now condescend upon any of them, except one from Professor Wilson for the best poem on the Covenanters.' There is something piquant in the thought of Robert McCheyne as a favourite pupil of Christopher North, the gentle and delicate lad conquering the esteem and affection of the bluff and leonine and boisterous author of the *Noctes Ambrosianæ*, who in the irony of things was then Professor of Moral Philosophy in Edinburgh.

The blank-verse eulogy of the Covenanters scarcely rises, it must be confessed, above the pedestrian levels of most University poems. It has its background in the abortive insurrection of 1666 and the pathos and tragedy of Rullion Green, though there is no attempt to abide by the historical

---

2. The proper Gaelic name of this sheet of water, which is very beautiful, pear-shaped, lying in a hollow, and surrounded by trees, is Lochan Oisinneach Mohr; but locally it is known as Loch Ooshnie or Oshnie. It is found midway among the hills between Dunkeld and Kirkmichael.

facts. It depicts a conventicle in a hollow of the Pentland
Hills, and the coming of the dragoons, and the capture and
imprisonment and subsequent martyrdom of the preacher.
He is sent, in Lauderdale's mocking language, to glorify God
in the Grassmarket; and 'see with how bold a step he mounts
the direful scaffold' – see 'his lofty mien, his stately form,
his eyes so calm and resolute'. With Hugh Mackail's Farewell and Welcome, *Ave atque Vale*, on his lips, he soars from
the contumelies and oppressions of the earth to the city which
makes melody for simple joy of heart.

> But now, all ye created things,
> Farewell! Thou glorious sun, farewell! Thy rays
> Shall light on me no more, nor any heat.
> Farewell, thou blessed Book! Thou wast through life
> Mine only comfort; thou art all my strength
> In death. Farewell, all friends and earthly joys!
> Believing, preaching, praying, all farewell!
> Welcome, grim death! Thrice welcome, endless bliss!
> Welcome, ye beckoning angels, bearing robes
> Purer and whiter than the drifted snow!
> Welcome, thou precious crown! Welcome, thou harp
> Of brightest gold, whose chords I soon shall strike
> In heavenly measures to the praise of Him
> Who died for me! Welcome, Thou Lamb of God,
> Thou joy and portion of my weary soul,
> Which shall endure through all eternity!

But before he passed into the Divinity classes of the University, to sit at the feet of men like Dr. Chalmers and Dr.
David Welsh, the greatest change of all had come to Robert
McCheyne. He was born of water and of the Spirit. His soul
received the regeneration of God, and his life left the natural
region for the supernatural.

'He was always a boy of the most amiable, I may even say noble, disposition' – it is the verdict of the sober-spoken and reticent father. 'I never found him guilty of a lie, or of any mean or unworthy action; and he had a great contempt for such things in others. I hardly recollect an instance of my having to inflict personal chastisement upon him.' Yet, blameless and beautiful as his demeanour was, he was not religious in the quick and penetrative and supreme sense of the word; after the light broke, he acknowledged that he had been 'a stranger to grace and to God'.

One turns back to the scrapbook to which allusion has been made, and which photographs for us the undergraduate as well as the schoolboy. It contains the essays done for his Latin and Greek professors; the speeches which he addressed to his fellows in the Academic Society, on the virtue of early rising, or on the rectitude and bravery of refusing rather than of accepting a challenge; and the valedictory verses, read at the closing meetings in two or three successive sessions, before the same kindly audience of young men. Some of these verses moralize in graceful and pensive rhythm – and Horace can do as much, with his *Eheu fugaces anni labuntur*! – over the remorseless flight of time, and the need for diligence and labour before the black night falls and says, 'Too late!'

Ah me! How the fast-fleeting years slip away,
    Like the sad silent flow of a river!
Even virtue their resolute course cannot stay;
For fair brows grow wrinkled, and wise heads grow grey,
    And the Grave is as greedy as ever.
Twelve moons have gone by since we last said Adieu:
    How much does their circuit embrace!

How many sweet harps have been severed in two,
And well-beloved voices and forms that we knew
   Have gone to their cold resting-place! ...

Up then, and be stirring! Let's work whilst 'tis day,
   For soon shall come darkness and sorrow.
Up, up! Let us handle the plough whilst we may,
Unswerving, undaunted, pursuing our way:
   We never may see a To-morrow.

But that is all. There is no deeper or diviner note. On the fly-leaf at the commencement of this book, the minister of St Peter's has inscribed the stern sentence: *Dum relego scripsisse pudet* – 'When I read again its contents, I am ashamed that ever I wrote them.' Well, they are innocent enough. But they have not been cleansed or kindled by the glowing stone from the heavenly altar; and to the man who, day in and day out, was led in triumph behind the chariot-wheels of Christ, they seemed pitifully inadequate. 'He was of a lively turn' – let us consult his father again; nobody has a better right to speak – 'and, during the first two or three years of his attendance at the University, he turned his attention to elocution and poetry and the pleasures of society rather more perhaps than was altogether consistent with prudence. His powers of singing and reciting were at that time very great, and his company was courted on that account more than was favourable to graver pursuits.' The spiritual awakening was still in the future. The vision tarried.

But when he was eighteen years of age, the wind blew on him out of that quarter where Christ is. Shall we say that it was a wind from a biting and arctic North rather than the soft South which breathes upon a bank of violets? As in many another instance, the sharp discipline of affliction was instrumental in working the transforming change. The family circle, so perfectly united and so singularly happy, was broken.

First, in April 1831, William McCheyne, having finished his training in medicine, received an appointment from the East India Company as doctor in the 54th Regiment of Native Infantry, and left Edinburgh for Bombay and Nasirabad, then a long way farther distant from the shores of Scotland than they are today.

Three months later a more shattering blow fell. On the 8th of July, David, Robert's eldest brother, died at the age of twenty-six. The end had been foreseen. Walking among the English lakes, and over the mountains of Cumberland and Westmorland, he had caught a cold from which he could not shake himself free, and which fastened more and more firmly and ineradicably on a frame which was never physically robust. So those who loved him better than they loved themselves had watched him slipping daily from their grasp. But, at the last, the anguish was as poignant, and the loss as desolating, as if the blow had descended in a moment.

David Thomas McCheyne was the pride of his home, and it seemed poor and empty when it was robbed of his presence. The father missed him sorely. He had himself planned and supervised his education; and, comparing him afterwards with his brothers, he declared that he was 'by far the best classical scholar of the three'. Like the older man, he had chosen the profession of law; and, after serving for five years in the Queen Street office as an apprentice, he was admitted a Writer to the Signet, and continued to assist his father in his business. He was Robert's willing and capable tutor during the boy's High School days, and when he was attending the Arts classes in college; and the lad leaned on him, and looked up to him with implicit trust. They were alike in vivaciousness of temperament. Two 'Epistles to Bob' can be read, which afford proof at once of David's cheerful good humour and of the strength of the tie which knit him with his younger brother. One is headed, 'Edinburgh, the 7th of June, at nearly 10 o'clock forenoon'; and this is its exordium –

> Bob, for the love you bear me,
> You must get up immediately,
> And seek the Post Office in haste:
> You know the road – *tam melius est*.

Arrived at his destination, the messenger must have no scruple about making his wants distinctly known.

> Then roar as if in Highland fashion,
> 'Anything for McCheyne and MacGlashan?'
> Or, on a sweetly soft voice fixing,
> Thrice 'Queen Street Number Fifty-Six' sing.

But, in the concluding years of his short life, David McCheyne drank of the gladnesses which are highest and holiest. He 'became deeply impressed with eternal realities'. There was no mistaking the miracle of grace; it was demonstrated in everything which he said and did.

Robert especially was conscious of the new quality in his brother's character; their friendship was so perfect that whatever moved the one reacted inevitably on the other. And David yearned over him, and strove by his speech, his example, and his prayers to pilot him home to the peaceable habitation in which he had gained a safe anchorage for himself.

> How oft that eye
> Would turn on me with pity's tenderest look,
> And, only half-upbraiding, bid me flee
> From the vain idols of my boyish heart!

But although there were inward convictions and penitences, voices of the uneasy conscience and resolutions of the will which is almost persuaded, there was no committal of the soul just yet to its Good Physician. Not until David was called up and away to be with Christ, did Robert enter the sure road to the same 'Circle, Centre, and Abyss of blessings'.

The last hours of his brother's life were marked by conflicting experiences. There was a brief spell of darkness and fear when the disciple, like the Master on the cross, went out into the wilderness of dereliction. But that passed. The clear shining of the Sun dispelled the gloom, and the open gate of the City stood forth to view, and the pilgrim was aware of the trumpets sounding for him on the other side. Again his faith, as Henry Vaughan would say, was 'pure and steady'. He saw his goal, and he was glad to reach it. It was by means of this deathbed that the Spirit of God preached Jesus, in the victorious fashion that prevails over all obstacles, to the young man who was witness of its grief and glory.

His Diary bears evidence that each returning anniversary of David's home-going was the memorial of the great crisis in his own history. And in a letter to a friend, dated on the 8th of July, 1842, he wrote: 'This day eleven years ago I lost my loved and loving brother, and began to seek a Brother Who cannot die'. Seeking, he found. He left the shadows for the Truth. He knew, beyond question and debate, Him Whom he had believed.

Alike by human training and endowment, and by superhuman grace, Robert McCheyne was prepared now to run his errand and to finish his work. In moulding and inspiring that better Scotland which is escaping from the shades of the prison-house, he will do his share, and in a short time will fulfil a long time.

CHAPTER 3

A Sower Went Forth to Sow

Recently a congregation of Christian men and women in Korea experienced a new springtime of the Holy Ghost. But one of its members was absent from home when the benediction came. Returning, he found his kinsfolk in Christ dowered with a richer spirituality than they had known before or than he knew now. 'Tell me,' he begged a friend, 'what it is, and how I shall get it.'

And the friend answered, 'It is what Paul writes to Timothy, *Lifting up holy hands*. I lift up both my hands to God. And the left hand is full. It contains all that I possess, and all that I myself am: this I yield and surrender to Him. But the right hand is empty. It holds nothing that is mine; it is always receiving what He keeps for me and communicates to me.' The exegesis may not be that of an approved scholarship, but it is that of the best Christianity.

This was McCheyne's Christianity, after he forsook the precincts of the Temple for the innermost shrine. The empty hand was lifted up. 'Jehovah Tzidkenu', once 'nothing to me', was now 'my treasure and boast', 'my cable, my anchor, my breastplate and shield'. In his Diary, ten months after his brother's death, he wrote: 'Thou hast made me all that I am, and given me all that I have'. Henceforward he waited; he expected; he thirsted for more holiness, more illumination, more fitness for obedience and service. So prayer became the initial necessity of every day. 'I feel it is far better to begin with God,' he said, 'to see His face first, and to get my soul near Him before it is near another.' And, as habitually, he listened to hear what Christ revealed and commanded. His acquaintance with the Bible grew rapidly into a singular intimacy.

With some like-minded friends in the Divinity Hall he started an Exegetical Society. It met, during the session of the Theological classes, every Saturday morning at half-past six; and the aim of its members was to dig deep in the field of Scripture. He could consult the Hebrew of the Old Testament, Dr. Bonar testifies, as easily as many ministers consult the Greek of the New. It was not merely the student's enthusiasm for the mastery of his textbook; it was the child's craving for the bread from the Father's table. 'Humble purpose-like reading,' he held, was essential. 'What plant can be unwatered and not wither?' There was no doubt about the empty hand, panting after the wealth of the King's storehouses.

But, side by side with it, he lifted the hand that is full. 'O, for activity, activity, activity!' the Diary cries on a March day in 1833; from the outset he realized that zeal is the only temper appropriate to the business of religion. 'Write Robert a good advice, to pay some attention to his health,' the mother besought her doctor son; for, once Christ captured him, he gave himself and all his faculties unconditionally away. Almost immediately he set about Home Mission work in the stairs and closes of the Lawnmarket, the High Street, and the Canongate; and he upbraided himself that he had not done it sooner. 'I have admired the huge black piles of building, with their lofty chimneys breaking the sun's rays – why have I never ventured within? What imbedded masses of human beings are huddled together, unvisited by friend or minister? Awake, my soul!'[1]

He was dominated by the longing to be of use. His letters disclose it in arresting fashion. Not one of them, it can safely be affirmed, but contains some sentence in commendation of the Lord whose thrall he was, or some eager entreaty to his correspondent to seek the healing which Christ bestows. From the hour of his conversion he lived *sub specie æternitatis*. 'Time hastens forward; and this world, like this sheet, will soon be done': it was the admonition which he crowded, in that minute and exquisite handwriting of his, into the bottom of a foolscap page, addressed to his brother in India. It was the admonition which constrained him to devote his own feet and hands and brain and heart to a consecration, a labour, and a sacrifice which never were intermitted or relaxed.

---

1. In a Tract, published by Dr. Chalmers in 1835, on 'The Cause of Church Extension, and the Question shortly stated between Churchmen and Dissenters in regard to it', an Appendix, dealing with the 'Results of Statistical Surveys taken in various districts, especially of towns, for the purpose of ascertaining the Ecclesiastical State of the People', permits us to see McCheyne and some of his friends at their Home Mission work. Here are two entries taken from this Appendix; they appear under the heading, 'Edinburgh: Within the Royalty':

'A District in the same Parish (the Tolbooth) from the Castle to No. 529 High Street, on the North Side of the Castle Hill: Population, 418; Sittings, 59; Proportion, less than 1 in 7; Authority, Rev. John Thomson and Mr. Andrew Bonar';

'A District extending from Seaton's Close, No. 265, to Mid Common Close, including Riddle's Close, being partly in New Street Parish and partly in Leith Wynd Parish: Population, 346; Sittings, 47; Proportion, less than 1 in 7; Authority, Mr. Alexander N. Somerville and Mr. R. M. McCheyne, Students of Divinity.'

Yet do not let us suppose that these ardours bred an aloofness from the 'familiar matters of today', or a Pharisaism of spirit. The letters are indubitable witnesses to the contrary. The old playfulness persists in gleaming up through them. There is still an interest taken in what transpires in the world of politics; Robert, like Adam McCheyne, is Conservative in his leanings, though his views are unfolded with a sweeter reasonableness than his father sometimes shows: when, in the spring of 1835, the House of Commons votes against the Cabinet 'that the surplus revenue of the Irish Church shall be converted into general education money' – 'we have just been signing an address to the King to make him keep in his Tory ministers spite of the squall, and one to Sir Robert Peel telling him to keep up his heart'. The charm, too, which natural scenery always had for him, especially when its loveliness is of the soft and gentle sort, was reiterated more spontaneously than ever; he 'had a kind and quiet eye,' a friend said, 'which found out the living and beautiful in nature rather than the majestic and sublime.' And he was as fond as before of turning to account his skill in drawing, and many a letter is illustrated by a sketch which renders vivid what he describes. McCheyne's religion was the soul of his soul; but it was as far removed from asceticism and sourness as June with its green felicity is from drear-nighted December.

The years of student life drew to an end at last. Their second half had been characterized by a more assiduous diligence than their beginnings; for the Spirit's unction clarified and sharpened every energy of his being, and the intellect shared in the quickening as well as the heart.

At the close of the session in 1835 he passed, before a committee of the Presbytery of Edinburgh, the private trials exacted from those seeking licence to preach, and soon afterwards, before the same Presbytery, a portion of the more public trials. Of this examination, in New Testament Greek, in Church History, and in Systematic Theology, he wrote humorously to his brother, 'For a good hour Gordon, Bruce, Paul, Clason, Hunter, and Somerville, all heckled me, like so many terriers on a rat'; it is the mother who adds, as mothers will, 'We have heard that Dr. Chalmers was highly pleased, and all the other ministers.'

But the metropolitan Presbytery was 'lost', like Augustine in his pre-Christian days, 'in a multiplicity of things'; and it looked as if McCheyne's actual licence might be delayed. So, in conformity with a custom occasionally followed, he asked that he might be transferred to an ecclesiastical court not quite so hard-driven; and before the Presbytery of Annan, in the South Country where his relatives lived and he was well-known, he was examined in Hebrew, and delivered the five discourses[2] which had been prescribed to him. It was here that, on the 1st of July, 1835, he was licensed, and became, as he expressed it, 'a preacher of the gospel, an honour to which I cannot name an equal'.

Four months later, in the opening week of November, his real ministry had its commencement – that brief ministry of seven-and-a-half years, which stamped an indelible impress on Scotland.

In response to the invitation of Mr. John Bonar, he went to be his assistant in the parishes of Larbert and Dunipace, not far from Stirling and its lion-rock. It was a great diocese of 710 families, where there was abundant work waiting to be done. Larbert was noisy, grim, industrial, with villages

---

2. 'Five' is the father's number here; Dr. Bonar, perhaps more correctly, says 'three'.

clustering round where the coal-miners and iron-moulders lived; Dunipace, three miles distant, was rural and secluded, the home of shepherds and small farmers, and the young assistant, when he visited it first, 'was delighted to breathe the fresh air of upland scenery once more'. The field of labour was thus a curiously varied one, and the labourer was prepared to spend himself without stint.

On the Monday morning after his first Sabbath, he sat down to tell his father the occupations of the previous day. 'I preached here,' in Larbert, 'to a large congregation, on Isaiah 1, and, again, on Ezekiel 33:10, 11. I was very thankful when I got finished, for my preparation had been but slight.' But this was merely the prelude.

After the sermons, 'Mr. Campbell, of some place near Torwood', asked him to come up next day, to see one of his cottars who was dying. But there was plenty of time before Mr. Bonar could return from Dunipace, and 'I thought I would just go with him then, which I did'. On the way the talk was of Popery and the restoration of the Jews.

When they reached the cottage at Carbrook, it was to learn that old Archibald, in whose heart had been some good thing towards God, was newly dead. 'The evening was deliciously fine, not a cloud over the whole sky. The wind was hushed; the trees all quite embrowned with autumn leaves; Ben Ledi and the distant hills covered with sprinklings of snow. The sun had just set, and spread a mellow watery tinge over the scene. The little cottage was before us, and everything seemed congenial with the death of a Christian. The sun had entered its rest. The birds were going to their rest. The dead leaves were gone to their rest. It was the Sabbath day, when Christ entered into his rest. And it was Archibald Macleay's dying hour, when he entered into the rest remaining for the people of God. We went into the cottage, where I joined in prayer with the mother, daughter, two sons, and several neighbours.'

An hour subsequently, he was back in the manse at Larbert. Then he walked down to Carron with Mr. Bonar, to hear him preach in the school, which he did 'with great effect and plain common-sense power for an hour and a half'. At night, 'we went to bed heartily tired'.

Such was the beginning, and all the sequel was as wakeful and unsparing. McCheyne had no indolent fibre either in his body or in his soul.

The two, the older man and his son in the faith, were well matched in determination to redeem the time. 'I am more and more pleased with Mr. Bonar for a Bishop,' Robert McCheyne records in the letter we have quoted. A week later he writes, 'His fault is secrecy, but he is opening up every day'. Two months afterwards he praises 'his inimitable way with children – he possesses a wonderful power of interesting them'. About this time Eliza was on a visit to her brother; and she sums up Mr. Bonar with the graphicness and decision of phrase which distinguish her. 'The minister was very tired, having visited no less than twenty-eight families. He seems a very active, pushing, driving man, very peculiar, very zealous, quite wrapped up in his parish. He spoke everything that was kind of Robert.'

The place sorely required both of the swift-footed messengers of Christ. The evil results of the long reign of Moderatism were palpable on every side. 'The people are savages for ignorance,' McCheyne reported; and again, 'There is very little of the work of God visible'; and yet again, 'I never knew till I came here what a curse a bad minister must be, and what a blighting desolation he casts around him, like the sirocco withering up the green life of faith, and giving no life to any'. He mourned over 'the heathens of Carron and Kinnairds'. He wished that the Church Commissioners could make trial of a single day's visiting in 'this beehive of a parish'; it would be a lesson to them not to 'cast the burden of so many souls on one set of shoulders'. He was amazed as well as saddened by the Cimmerian darkness; until he had attempted to grope through it and to grapple with it, he could not have conceived it possible. 'She is so deaf,' he wrote in June, 1836, about a woman he had just seen, 'that she says hardly anybody can make her hear. She is so blind that she cannot read. She is so cold and careless that she does not want to know. And she is so old that she will very soon die. She knew that Jesus had shed His blood. But when I asked her why, she said that really her memory was so bad she could not tell, but that her husband "used to be a grand man at the Buiks".'

McCheyne had wished to be a Foreign Missionary; but among his 'sweet colliers', as he designates them with quaint affection, there was a paganism as dense as that of Central Africa; and early and late he strove to dissipate and vanquish it.

His sermons, and often there were three of a Sabbath, dealt with the primary evangelic facts. He expounded a man's need and God's supply, sin in its guilt and contamination, judgment in its certainty and its awfulness, Christ in His power and His love. He could be very practical and pointed, leaving, as Pericles did, troublesome *kentra* to rankle in the minds of his auditors.

So it happened with Major Dundas of Carron Hall, who 'always speaks out what comes uppermost'. After the lecture one morning – it had treated of the Parable of the Sower – this was his verdict: 'I congratulate you, Mr. McCheyne, on being the only minister I have heard tell the people their faults.' The preacher confessed that the compliment pleased him; not in itself, because the speaker abounded in eulogistic words, but because it gave him some hope that the hammer had struck the nail on the head: was it not undeniable that, now and then, the Major had been in his thoughts, while he published that day the truth with which God had entrusted him?

But the chief reason why his messages went home was that each had been delivered to himself before it was carried to the people. Like Bunyan, he spoke 'what he felt, what he smartingly did feel'; and his preaching, in his biographer's suggestive language, 'was the development of his soul's experience and the giving out of the inward life'. In manner, it must have been fluent and untrammelled almost from the outset. His discourses were written with care from introduction to application; or, if time for this was not forthcoming, the course of their thoughts and arguments was detailed with conscientious particularity, as one might travel from tree to tree in an avenue, or from headland to headland along the coastline portrayed on a map.

But in public the sermons and addresses were never read from manuscript. After a few months, he gave over trying even to commit their sentences and paragraphs to memory. He was content to familiarize himself with the ideas and the illustrations; the expression was left to God's guidance and the impulses of the soul at the moment he confronted the congregation. When he 'saw the folk' and 'the Word was on him to deliver', then 'with a rush the intolerable craving shivered throughout him'.

How he found the outgate into this ease and readiness of utterance he explains in one of his home-letters; its date is July 12, 1836. 'On my way to Dunipace last Sabbath, I happened to be going rather fast on Tully; and my sermons both slipt out. I never missed them till I got to the church. One of them I had scarcely read over. However, there was nothing for it but going straight on. I got over the forenoon with some exertion; but, fearing for the afternoon, I sent back a messenger to Larbert, thinking I had left the manuscript on my table. In vain! So I had to preach away, and did much better than usual. Man's extremity is God's opportunity.' It was a happy providence, in spite of its frowning face; and perhaps it was not the least of the services which his good pony – 'Tullia' on state occasions, but 'Tully' more colloquially and habitually – who canters delightfully through the correspondence, and who is 'not a majestic creature but a useful beast', was able to render her master.

The week was as brimful as the Sabbath with duties undertaken and done. All through his ministry it was patent that McCheyne attached no less importance to the visitation of his people from house to house than to their instruction from the pulpit. Nothing can be more systematic or painstaking – nothing has spoken more poignantly to one ministerial reader of them – than those notebooks which reveal his tireless and methodical diligence in visiting. He has made it an exact science: there are such precision and perfection of knowledge, such discrimination of character, such watchfulness over individual souls. Yes, an exact science; yet with no coldness and no hardness in its mathematical accuracy. Behind each of these significant entries we catch sight of a man of God adjuring a brother-immortal to pause and consider these things which pertain to his peace, or wrestling in prayer for him with strong cryings and tears. Let us copy out a few of the entries, premising that what is printed here in italics appears in the notebook in crimson ink and refers to the Scripture which the visitor read and expounded. We may accompany him from door to door of the miners' village of Red Row. There are about fifty houses in it, and in the course of a day he makes acquaintance with twelve or fifteen of these.

'John Hunger, No. 22. He, not at home. She, stout woman with sensible face. Spoke of her four bairns dead; three beside her. Visit, 14 July, 1836. *I stand at door and knock.* Altogether a decent woman. Husband to be at meeting.'

'James Rankin, No. 23. He at work. Wife hoarse-speaking, attentive, understanding body. He, son of Betty Denovan. Two children; three dead. Visit, 14 July, 1836. *Story of sick child.* Spoke with some plainness.'

'Alexander MacLuckie, No. 24. Red-haired man; honest, inquiring face. Wife, clever body. Four girls. Visit, 14 July, 1836. Asked the little girls questions, directed all to them. *Suffer the children to come*; with application to parents.'

'Alexander Hunter, No. 39. Intelligent man. Met with wife in Robert's (No. 20). Decent-like family; boy and girl; have lost three. Spoke of Davy's lamp. Visit, 21 July. *Treasure hid.* He recommended prayers for the workers underground.'

'Widow Hunter, No. 40. Wicked face, but old body has had much trouble. Daughter lame. Visit, 21 July. *Lost sheep.* Spoke plain. She spoke grateful things, but felt them not. Invited me not to pass the door.'

'Peter Rae, No. 44. Ill-looking man. Hard, hard woman. A large family of mocking lasses. Visit, July 21. *One thing needful*, pardon and new heart. Tried to break this northern iron.'

Thus the pregnant memoranda run on; for he was a *Seelenführer*, a seeker of weary souls, who never abated his eagerness or abandoned his quest. Only sometimes, when there was sickness in a house, the page delineates an urgency even more insistent. Many visits have to be chronicled then, and the result of each must be estimated and weighed. The spiritual progress or decline of the sufferer is diagnosed with a physician's sense of responsibility; there is an unfeigned gladness over any hint of healing, a weeping pain over the development of the mortal disease. McCheyne feared to let slip an opportunity.

Once, on an August evening, walking to Torwood schoolhouse, he came upon a band of gypsies, sitting round their fire of wood; and he preached to them about the lost sheep –

But one was out on the hills away,
    Far off from the gates of gold; –

'the children were very attentive, and the old people a little touched'. If he had passed by, he might not have encountered the homeless wanderers again.

Through every hour and in every company the recollection haunted him, *Behold, now is the acceptable time; behold, now is the day of salvation.* 'There is a tide in the affairs of grace,' he wrote in one of his letters, 'which, taken at the flood, leads on to safety; omitted, all the voyage of our souls is cast in shallows and in miseries.' As much as in him lay, he persuaded men to take advantage of that blessed tide.

And all the while that he refused to spare himself, his health was delicate and fragile. From an early period he carried in him the tendency to consumption. When things were favourable, the trouble was quiescent; but the least provoca-

tion induced it to assert itself in annoying and hampering
ways. He was enrolled among the volunteers and athletes of
Christ who have prayed for 'a short life in the saddle' rather
than 'long life by the fire', and to whom their Lord has
granted their request. Once at least, during his ten months in
Larbert, he had a serious breakdown, and for some weeks
was forced to abandon his work; what a joy he felt when,
'well wrapped up in his great coat', he could venture out
again! 'I hope,' he said, 'God is going to change severities
into mercies.'

The mother in Edinburgh had an anxious mind about her
son. She kept sending him comforts he was not always willing to accept; 'the shirts and flannels,' he told her, 'are works
of supererogation, and therefore by no means orthodox.' The
difference was complete between the old Queen Street or
Hill Street home and the solitary room that was his lodging
in what Eliza called mischievously 'the celebrated Mrs. Graham's'; but in Mrs. Graham's room he saw a goodly heritage
and a wealthy place. He made merry over its furnishings. 'In
dimensions it is about 16 by 10. But as it contains a bed, two
chests of drawers, three tables, and six immense chairs, with
my two trunks, locomotion is rather impeded. I will attempt
to draw it some other time, as I think the subject abundantly
worthy of the pencil of Hogarth.' But the landlady was
friendly and kind, and he was well pleased with his abode.

Nothing was farther from his desire than the plenty the
world can give. On a spring day Mr. Bonar and he rode to
Airth, to examine the parish school. The manse, he decided,
'is altogether too sweet and pretty, and a man can hardly live
there without saying, "This is my rest." I don't think,' he
went on, 'ministers' manses should ever be so beautiful.'
His '16 by 10' chamber satisfied him better; and how he

hallowed it and magnified it by his prayers and praises! It was a house of God and a gate of heaven.

Then the call came to a church and parish of his own. McCheyne found the sphere with which we associate his name, as surely as we associate Samuel Rutherfurd with Anwoth, Richard Baxter with Kidderminster, and Charles Simeon with Cambridge.

CHAPTER 4

In Labours More Abundant

Writing to his father and mother on the 30th of June, 1836, Robert McCheyne makes reference for the first time to the possibility of his being called to Dundee. 'As for concern about the result,' he says, 'I have none. The choosing is all in His higher hand, who turns the hearts of men like the rivers of waters. It is curious my two greatest intimates being made my rivals. I have no doubt we will contend with all humility, in honour preferring one another. If the people have any sense, they will choose Andrew Bonar, who, for learning, experimental knowledge, and all the valuable qualities of a minister, outstrips all the students I ever knew.' It is a happy enfranchisement which true friends enjoy from the vexing miseries of suspicion and envy. When Christ is Chiefest in their loyalty, they had rather have a companion crowned than win the garland and diadem themselves.

A book might be dedicated to the subject of McCheyne's friendships. He was the central figure in a group of young preachers, whose ministries had a profound influence in evangelizing the Church and the land. Most of them spoke and laboured for long years after he had gone to God; but they never forgot him, or parted with that note of heavenliness and of urgency which he helped to give their dialect and their character.

There was James Grierson of Errol, in whose manse he

stayed on the night before his ordination in Dundee.

There was James Hamilton of Abernyte, and soon of Regent Square in London; 'when I compare myself with him,' James Hamilton said, 'I see what sinful trifling much of my ministry has been.'

There was Alexander Moody-Stuart[1] of Edinburgh; how glad he was when his father and mother forsook the Moderatism of St. Stephen's for the clearer gospel and the warmer Christianity of St. Luke's, and when, ere long, the father became an elder in Moody-Stuart's congregation!

There was Robert Macdonald of Blairgowrie; 'let me hear from you soon,' he pleaded in October, 1837, 'for a letter from R. McC. is peculiarly refreshing.'

A little later, there was John Milne of Perth, gentle, saintly, apostolic; 'they both walked nimbly and erectly,' Horatius Bonar writes, 'moving with an agility that spoke of inward joy.'

There was Horatius Bonar himself, then and for years afterwards minister of Kelso, to whom Scotland and the Christian world are debtors for his psalms and hymns and spiritual songs.

There were others who are not so well known, but who turned many to righteousness and will shine as the stars for ever, like Mr. Cumming of Dumbarney and Mr. Cormick of Kirriemuir.

And then there were his 'two greatest intimates', who were his rivals when the people of St. Peter's looked for a teacher and a shepherd.

One was Alexander Neil Somerville, with whom he had

---

1. In McCheyne's correspondence Dr. Moody-Stuart is spoken of simply as 'Moody'; the 'Stuart' was added subsequently when he married Miss Stuart of Annat.

been at school and college in Edinburgh, and who followed him as assistant in Larbert and Dunipace; 'perhaps,' this friend wrote to him once – 'perhaps we may get a lodging near each other in the golden streets of the New Jerusalem'. For most of his life Somerville was minister of Anderston Church in Glasgow, where his earliest text was, *For Zion's sake I will not hold my peace, and for Jerusalem's sake I will not rest, until the righteousness thereof go forth as brightness, and the salvation thereof as a lamp that burneth* – a self-revealing text, for, as it was truly said, there was something of the *burning lamp* in all his ministry of fifty-two years, and it never lost the radiant and ruddy heat in which it began.

The fact is that its closing period was its most ardent. Then, like John Wesley, Alexander Somerville took the whole world for his parish, and went everywhere publishing the glad tidings of God. In Spain, in India, in Australasia, in France and Italy and Germany and Russia, in South Africa, in Greece and Western Asia, through the Scottish Highlands and Islands, among the Jews of Western Europe, the old man eloquent carried the blazing torch of Christ's truth and love.

The final scene was in keeping with all that preceded. When he lay dead he was dressed in what may be called his 'working clothes', the suit he had last preached in. His hair was brushed out, and the velvet cap he wore in the house was put on. He looked as if he might be taking a short sleep before going on a new errand of grace. It was an injunction he had laid on his children to bury him in his ordinary dress; and he wanted, he added, to have a little mud on his boots.

The other intimate was Andrew Alexander Bonar, brother of Horatius and cousin of McCheyne's 'bishop' in Larbert, biographer in a few years' time of Robert McCheyne himself. Andrew Bonar was dearer than any of the rest; and, although each had his own spiritual aroma and distinctive appeal, the pre-eminence was his by right. His scholarship was fuller and more accurate than his friend's. His religion was as supreme, 'the fountain-light of all his day'. And he was as human as he was godly, genial and brother-like, with a refreshing humour that played beautifully and reverently even about sacred things, and with a lovableness which captivated every one.

His very dreams were of that invisible kingdom from which he never wandered in his waking hours. Once it is: 'I thought in my sleep I tried to indite a new Greek word, something like κυριοσ and καιροσ, to express the Lord's seasonable mercies.' Or it is: 'Dreamed last night that I was dying, and, at the moment I seemed about to depart, I saw presented to me words that spoke of Christ's complete salvation. *Potentissimus*, I remember, was one, and it made me think upon Him able to save to the uttermost. There was another that spoke of His work for sinners, but I forget the word. It was a pleasant dream.' Or again: 'Last night I dreamed I got such a view of God's kindness and benefits to me, that for some time my throat felt choked. I could find no way of giving utterance to my overwhelming feeling of wonder.' And yet once more, twenty years after the comrade of his youth had winged his flight to the hills of frankincense: 'Last night I had been dreaming a great deal of being with McCheyne, Alexander Thain, and some others. Is the Lord wishing by this to excite in me more intense conviction? More prayer? More faith? More zeal? More love?'

In 1836, Andrew Bonar was assistant in Jedburgh. Two years thereafter, he came from helping Mr. Candlish in St. George's, Edinburgh, to be ordained over the quiet country parish of Collace in Perthshire. There he was near enough to Robert McCheyne for the friends to see each other often, and to strengthen one another's hands in God.

St. Peter's in Dundee, which claimed the probationer whom Larbert would fain have kept, was a new church. The town had been rapidly increasing; in 1835 its population numbered 51,000 souls. But in its church buildings, Kirk-of-Scotland and Dissenting, there was accommodation for no more than 18,000; and the discrepancy had begun to weigh heavily on those who had the welfare of the community at heart.

Among these were the office-bearers of St. John's Church, of which Mr. Roxburgh was minister. Impelled by a wish to remedy what was so grievously amiss, they resolved to 'erect a chapel in the north-west end of the Hawkhill'; selecting this quarter because it seemed the most necessitous, because it was farthest from the existing places of worship, and because it was inhabited entirely by members of the working class. By May of 1836 the 'plain and substantial' house of God – the epithets are those of the circular that invited subscriptions for its building – was finished; all except the spire, whose construction had to tarry for three years more.

Then the kirk-session of St. John's set itself to discover a spiritual overseer for the new charge, determining, however, as wise men would, that the congregation must have the conclusive word in the matter. The advice of Dr. Chalmers, Dr. Welsh, and Mr. Candlish was asked; and the trusted leaders of Evangelicalism recommended the three preachers whom we know – Alexander Somerville, Andrew Bonar, and Robert McCheyne – together with three others of kindred temper, Mr. White of Edinburgh, Mr. Dymock of Liberton, and Mr. Gibson of Glasgow. When the time arrived for the con-

gregation's choice, McCheyne was preferred by a large majority; and on the 24th November, 1836, he was ordained.

On the following Sabbath he delivered his first sermon
from the pulpit that is linked unbreakably with his name.
The text was his Master's text in Nazareth, a verse to which
he was accustomed to return on succeeding anniversaries of
the day: *The Spirit of the Lord God is upon me; because the
Lord hath anointed me to preach good tidings unto the meek;
He hath sent me to bind up the broken-hearted, to proclaim
liberty to the captives, and the opening of the prison to them
that are bound.* It was prophetic of the future that, under this
initial sermon, some hearts were awakened to the vision of
the world which is unseen, and on this man and that the
morning broke which is never overtaken by sunset and night.
Week after week, within the walls of St. Peter's, the gracious
signs were repeated. In his Monday letter to his parents, the
minister's continual aspiration is, 'I hope something may have
been done'; or, 'I trust good was done for Eternity'. And
from his pen the words were not a conventional and decora-
tive euphemism. They uttered his deepest prayer, and they
had numerous fulfilments.

From the first the church was full. Within the boundaries
marked out for the parish there was a population of 3,400,
but hearers came from other parts of the town and from the
country round; till usually the building was crowded by about
1,100 people. They sat on the steps of the pulpit; they stood
often in the passages and corners of the edifice. And no words,
as James Hamilton wrote to Andrew Bonar, could preserve
the atmosphere which permeated the place and surrounded
the speaker, 'the Bethel-like sacredness of Sabbaths and Communions', 'the peculiar impression of "God is here".'

It was not the magnetism of mere oratory which drew

those crowds. McCheyne had much of the poet in his nature, and his preaching could never be commonplace. There was pathos in it; there was winningness; there was fire. From everything frigid and formal it was far withdrawn. Life quivered in its utterances, and passed through them to the men and women who heard. But it could easily be criticized and his warmest friends were not unaware of its faults. When James Hamilton listened to it first, he did not like the voice; he thought that the 'slow and almost singing cadence' was affectation. The preacher's father, too, lamented the change in that voice, 'once so melodious'. It 'soon became cracked and broken,' he says, 'long discourses, sometimes three in a day, during the delivery of which he was naturally much excited, wrought mischievous effects.' Thus, from the rhetorician's point of view, there were blemishes not so difficult to discern.

Yet, considered solely from this side, it was singularly effective preaching. The style had always the charm of perfect lucidity; it was transparent, like the crystal waters of a lake into which the observer gazes and sees the pebbles and grasses at the bottom. As invariably, it had the merit of definite purposefulness; long as the discourses were, there were no superfluous garniture and no deliberate gilding; the illustrations, a listener testifies, were 'not flowers for the fancy but arrows for the conscience'.

But the potent and manifest attraction of St. Peter's lay elsewhere than in any externalities. It lay in the simplicity, freeness, and sufficiency of the gospel which was proclaimed from its pulpit; in the unearthly airs and powers of the Spirit of God that breathed and blew through the prayers and the sermons; and in the personality of the preacher. His outward presence satisfied the eye. He was tall, slender, of fair com-

plexion, regular and handsome in feature, pleasant to look
upon as young David coming from the sheepfold to be
anointed king. And, behind the face and the words, the soul
was more constraining and more compelling. Here, everyone felt, was a true ambassador of Christ and a man filled
unto all the fullness of God. In the herald and servant the
people saw and heard the Lord. 'Certainly He was there with
them.'

Two thick notebooks in quarto remain from those introductory years in Dundee. Their pages are occupied with the
preliminary sketches of discourses, many of which Mc-
Cheyne wrote out afterwards more amply and exactly. If in
his public speech he could let himself go, in the thinking and
the writing which led up to the speech he was disciplined
and diligent. For the Thursday night prayer-meeting as well
as for the preaching of the Sabbath he got himself ready by
patient study; from point to point the outline is traced of
what he meant to say even at this more familiar gathering.
And when it is the high solemnity of the Lord's Supper that
is in view, he is busier still. Not only is the Action Sermon
delineated in its main and subordinate divisions, but we learn
how he intends to 'fence the tables', and the scope and tenor
of the addresses before and after Communion. His liberty of
prophesying was not an unchartered freedom. It had been
prefaced, and it was limited and controlled, by quiet meditation, by illuminating prayer, and by steadfast toil.

It is hard to summarize the contents of the two quartos;
they hold infinite riches. There are the schemes and charts
of lectures on those chapters of Chronicles which narrate
the story of the building and consecration of Solomon's Temple; on different Psalms and Parables; on the first Epistle of
Peter; on the Epistles to the Seven Churches. There are ser-

mons in miniature, whose texts and subjects are drawn from almost every section of the Old Testament and the New. There are quotations from the books he has been reading: Cotton Mather's *Life of John Eliot*, John Flavel's meditations, Young's *Night Thoughts*, Jonathan Edwards's resolutions and tracts and treatises, Luther on *The Galatians*, Bunyan's *Jerusalem Sinner Saved*. There is his 'Division of the Bible, so the whole may be read over every two months or every month'. There are careful Biblical studies: on Judas the betrayer, on the dress of the High Priest and its significance, on prayer, on the doctrine of the Holy Spirit.

As we travel through the volumes, lovingly and lingeringly, the preacher himself lives again before us.

We see how unalloyed and absolute is his satisfaction with Christ; to that Pole his thought and his heart, like the needle in the compass, are always quivering back. We learn that it is impossible for him to forget Calvary, or the God of Calvary, who, 'rather than His justice should be stained, did stain the ɣ *R.. 3:24* Cross', and rather than His love should miss its end, refused to spare His Son.

We are rebuked by the writer's faithfulness and zeal; no Christianity contents himself but one which rules him through and through, and no poorer Christianity, he insists, should content his people; so his message to them, one Sabbath, is the message of God to Israel through Hosea, *Behold, I will hedge up thy way with thorns, and make a wall, that she shall not find her paths; and then shall she say, I will go and return to my first Husband, for then was it better with me than now*.

We are moved and awed by his importunities with the careless and sinful. He can use the surgeon's scalpel to probe the ugly wounds of the soul. He does not shrink from unveiling the severities of the Word. His text may be, *If any man love not the Lord Jesus Christ, let him be anathema*; or it is that 'dolorous blast' of Ezekiel, *A sword, a sword is sharpened and also furbished*. But, generally, he prefers the note which is wooing and persuasive. It is Christ's *Come* which he sounds in the hearing of the heavy-laden; and oftenest his voice is not that of wind or earthquake or fire – it is the voice of gentle stillness. The Lord hath anointed him to preach good tidings; He hath sent him to proclaim the opening of the prison to them that are bound.

The Thursday prayer-meeting was a new thing in the religion of the town. It was so large that it was held in the church itself; we read of eight hundred as sometimes attending. A special benediction rested on it; the wings of the Spirit lay close and warm then about speaker and hearers. 'The Thursday meetings are dear to me,' he said; 'they will be remembered in Eternity with songs of praise.'

In those informal gatherings he was frank and unfettered. He laid aside that 'new silk gown', of which he wrote to his mother, 'It is so large and handsome that you would take me for a Bishop at the very least', and arrayed in which, as he told his father, he 'ascended the pulpit with a rustling like the leaves of Vallombrosa'. With the gown other stiffnesses and statelinesses, though McCheyne was never much cumbered by these, were gone. He dealt with subjects more varied in their range than he discussed on Sabbaths in the congregation. He unbarred the floodgates and let the river of his affections stream forth; he drew very near to the people, and they to him. And there was One who came nearer still, the Lord who confirms and comforts, teaches and saves.

Other agencies rendered the congregation's life yet more intelligent and spiritual. There was the Bible Class; six months after his ordination he speaks of its members as numbering 170 girls and 70 young men. To his brother, home now from India and somewhat of an invalid, he describes, in February, 1838, one of his courses of instruction. 'It is what I call the Geographical Method. I give them out some place, such as the Sea of Galilee, and bid them look up the passages that refer to it in the Bible. Then I draw a map of it in chalks upon a board, as we used to do at the High School. Then I teach them where all the places are; and read descriptions of it from Josephus, the Jewish historian, and from modern travellers, like Burckhardt and Buckingham. Then I go over the parts of the Bible which relate to it, and illustrate them by the geographical positions and by the descriptions read. I find this very interesting to myself, and they are quite delighted with it.' He appends a sketch of the Sea of Galilee with its towns and villages, and adds, 'You must not smile at my fine map-making'.

But more intimate and sacred were his classes for young communicants, and his personal interviews with the young communicants themselves. There were thirty-seven of them when the first Sacramental Sabbath arrived; 'it is thought a great number in this place'. He was very brotherly and kind with these applicants for admission to the Holy Table; but he was jealous of its sanctity and earnest for their welfare. One of the Fathers writes that, at the Communion in the Upper Room, eleven of the guests ate the Lord with the bread, while one ate onlythe bread with the Lord: it was McCheyne's aspiration that those who joined the Church should be kinsfolk of the eleven, and not of the one. While nothing was more tender than his talk with them, nothing was more searching. 'This is the season,' he declared, 'when a minister comes to know the fruits of his ministry.' Many were the discover-

ies he made in these heart-to-heart conversations – many the
assurances he received that through him the Friend of men
was finding His wayward children, to awaken, to forgive,
and to bless.

His visitation of his members was pursued in Dundee as
indefatigably as it had been in Larbert. But in the crowded
'lands' and tenements of a manufacturing town, where the
toilers are herded together, the task appeared endless, and he
never felt as if it were finished and done. His visiting book
is as wedded to accuracy and thoroughness as before; but it
has its pictorial supplements now. When he has gone over
sixteen or eighteen homes lying in near proximity to one
another, and has noted the names of their inmates, and his
own impressions of them, he inserts a kind of topographical
or architectural plan, in which each family has its residence
properly indicated and placed; so that the minister will not
confound James Martin's door with Robert Moodie's, or cross
David Edward's threshold when he is really in quest of Margaret Penicuik's.

One class of his parishioners could always be certain of
an attention which recognized no limit and rose above all
fatigue – those whom illness had laid aside, or who were
soon to die.

Speaking to students of medicine, Dr. Stephen Paget reminds them that they practise their science and art on life
itself, and that, with such priceless material, an error may be
irreparable. 'Medicine,' he says, 'works in lives, and cannot
correct its proofs, or begin with a sketch, or waste its fabrics, or rehearse its effects, or use a model; and by a mistake
it injures not an image of life, but life.' 'That,' he goes on, 'is
why Medicine is not a fine art; it is not the art but the stuff
which is so fine. The doctor must interfere with that one

substance which is above all else in nature, the one texture, man, infinitely complex, infinitely precious. We touch heaven when we lay our hands on the human body.'[2] These were McCheyne's convictions. He was working in lives, in the stuff and substance whose complexity and preciousness are incalculable. He must beware of mistake, for mistake might be fatal. He touched heaven when he laid his hands on the human spirit. And if the spirit was approaching the verge and term of its earthly probation, if it was passing within the veil, his anxiety over it was multiplied sevenfold; he could not do enough for its healing and help. In Dundee he has a book which is devoted exclusively to this department of his ministry. On the page at the beginning he has written the inscription:

Jesus—
I was sick, and ye visited Me.
Believers—
*When saw we Thee sick or in prison,
and came unto Thee?*
Jesus—
*Verily, I say unto you, Inasmuch as ye have done it
unto one of the least of these My brethren,
ye have done it unto Me.*

Shall we extract a single page from the book itself, to show us how a good physician goes about his most delicate and critical work? This is one of the earliest:

Thomas Tyrie, Step Row, lowest 'land'. Ill of consumption for five years. Takes opium.

---

2. *Confessio Medici*, pp. 84, 85.

Visited, 12 Dec., 1836. – Debate about hell and annihilation. *Lost sheep.*[3] He attentive. Has read his Bible, rather to cavil at it. Neighbours in.

Visited, 19 Dec. – Has been asking often for me. *Lost piece*. He still attentive, and consents to the whole truth.

Visited, 20 Dec. – *Prov. 1: Turn you at My reproof*. Sleepier than usual; yet 'corroborated' all, as he said.

Visited, 22 Dec. – *The Lord opened Lydia's heart*. More attentive. Said that great change had taken place, and spoke of his peace within during these two weeks. Still speaks through opium, but wonderfully sensible.

Visited, 28 Dec. – *Christ a Substitute*. Explained the whole gospel, and pressed it on him. Strangely sensible answers. Who knows but there may be some work of the Spirit here? He says that his views of his own heart and of Christ are both changed.

Visited, 31 Dec. – Found his cold remains wrapped up; and Margaret crying. Died on Friday morning, 30 Dec., before light; no one saw him die. Thus ends this short but interesting history. There was certainly a wonderful change in the man. He took to his Bible, before unread; spoke with interest of his soul and of the Saviour; was glad of my visits, and squeezed my hand always with affection. But whether there was a work of Grace the Day shall declare.

It is proof that at length the Church of Scotland was shaking itself free from the stifling incubus of Moderatism, that, within the first twelve months of his residence in Dundee, McCheyne was offered, three times over and from three different parishes, a new sphere of work. There were many who felt that he ought to have more restfulness and comfort than

---

3. Here, as before, the italics appear, in McCheyne's handwriting, in crimson ink, and indicate the Scriptural passages or truths which he expounded to the sick man.

he could hope to find in a freshly formed congregation which had yet to be shaped into stability and strength, or amongst the unceasing whirl and noise of factory wheels. His yearly stipend in St. Peter's was only £200; there were places, eager to gain him, which could give him far more. Moreover, that sensitive body of his, easily conquered by illness, might be built into robuster health in more favourable surroundings, away from the chimney smoke and from those overcrowded rooms and garrets where the mill-workers lived.

In January, 1837, it was Skirling in Peebles-shire which tempted him; in March, it was St. Leonard's in Edinburgh; and, in June, it was St. Martin's near Perth. Each had its attractions, but each was decisively refused. To Lady Carmichael of Castle Craig, who had written him for her husband, asking him to accept of Skirling, he replied in a long and very noble letter. He saw all the allurements of the country; but for him the path of duty was manifest, and he must go on walking under the dingy skies and along the hard pavements of the town.

'The advantages of the parish you offer me are indeed very great, in my case peculiarly so. The pecuniary emolument is remarkably handsome, and, all things considered, is nearly double the income I expect to receive in this place. The smallness of the parish, quite a parochial family, where I might exert my energies to the utmost without fear of injuring myself, would make the situation suitable to my somewhat delicate frame of body. The quietness and leisure that would be afforded me are most precious in my eyes, as they would enable me to prosecute the studies which here I can only sigh after in vain. The agricultural population would have answered my tastes exactly; for I know not a greater privilege than to carry the words of faith and love to the farm and the cottage-hamlet, to deal with plain unvarnished minds, to "allure to brighter worlds and lead the way".

'Still, dear Madam, I am here. I did not bring myself here. I did not ask to be made a candidate for this place. I was hardly willing to be a candidate. I did not expect success, nor was I in the least anxious for it; I was as happy at Larbert as the day was long. And yet God turned the hearts of this whole people toward me, like the heart of one man. I do not know that there was an individual among them discontented with my settlement. Is it presumptuous, then, to think that this call was not of man, neither by man, but from the Great Master Himself, just as plainly as if He had said to me, "This is your corner of the vineyard"? O no, I dare not leave this people.

'Some of my friends have said that the call which your confiding kindness has given me is another call of Providence; and, if the sphere were as wide as that which I now occupy, or as wide as to demand the whole energies of an ordinary mind, perhaps I would agree with them. But then, when I remember that I would be exchanging thousands for hundreds, that I would be leaving a Sabbath audience of 1100 for 150, I do not feel that I could ask God's blessing on the change. His favour is life; His loving-kindness is better than life. To be where He would have us, and to have the sunlight of His countenance shed upon all our paths, that is heaven upon earth, wherever our home may be, in a cottage or in a castle, or, with John, in a dungeon.

'I must rest in hope that He will bless me in the place which He has chosen for me, among the bustling artisans and the political manufacturers of Dundee. He who paid

His own and His disciple's tribute out of the fish's mouth will supply all my need. He will make my strength to be as my day is. He will make me a practical divine, which, after all, is better than a learned divine. And perhaps He will make this wilderness of chimney-tops to be green and beautiful as the garden of the Lord, a field which the Lord hath blessed.'

The outcome was the same in the other two cases, though they offered him a larger usefulness and a more exacting labour than Skirling could do. Mr. Nairne of Dunsinnan tried in vain to coax him to grant the people of St. Martin's a chance of listening to him; 'no minister should preach as a candidate,' he asserted categorically and immovably.

There were friendly foes of his own household whom he found it more difficult to resist and convince. His mother, longing that he should *prosper and be in health as his soul prospered*, would have had him accept Sir Thomas and Lady Carmichael's proposal. 'Dear Mamma,' he wrote, 'you must just make up your mind to let me be murdered among the lanes of Dundee, instead of seeing me fattening on the green glebe of Skirling. Perhaps it would have been very good for my frail body; but then, I fear, my soul would have turned sickly, and the most precious part would have withered. I would have felt myself a renegade, seeking my own, not the things which are Jesus Christ's.' The saints sometimes have a face like a flint and a heart like an adamant stone, even when their 'best beloved of all' are beseeching them to modify their fixity of purpose. So it was with Perpetua of Carthage in the early days; and so it was with Robert McCheyne.

He had his recompense soon. 'There is an awakened look about my people,' he records in the middle of June, immediately after he has said his definitive 'No' to Mr. Nairne and St. Martin's. Among the Radical weavers and the jute manufacturers, whose dinner-tables were marked by 'a great want of sentiment' – 'Bare facts go down best, the failing of a mill, the quantity of debt' – the gales were stirring that have their birth high and far in the invisible world. 'My sweet parish is a little paradise,' its minister said.

In the midst of the throng and accumulation of his activities, he kept his human sympathies awake.

He could conduct with his father a spirited debate over the ethics of Life Insurance: is it Christian? Is it in the line of the teaching of the New Testament? Is it according to the mind and will of Jesus? The Writer to the Signet was stout in his support of the affirmative; his son argued for the negative, and held to his belief in spite of everything that could be adduced on the opposite side; before he will abandon his opinion, Christ's word, *Lay not up treasures on earth*, must be amended into, *Lay up treasures in the Insurance Office*.

A few months later he was as keenly interested as his sister in the equipment of their house, in Strawberry Bank, on the Perth Road: the chairs his mother would have selected at twenty-seven shillings apiece are pronounced over-costly, and there is to be no French bed, which to all certainty will not correspond with the size of his small rooms.

Or he would throw much lively enjoyment into his recital of his experiences, as this narrative of 'a visitation day' will witness.

'Having warned thirteen families the night before, I girded myself for the combat and commenced. I met great kindness in every house, though there were only three or four that belonged to my church. Most were Old Light dissenters,[4] who have many truly godly people among them. One widow I came upon, who of children and grandchildren has twenty-five altogether; about a dozen were in the house. I went over all with great comfort, taking a rest in the middle. One woman offered me my dinner of 'sowens'[5], which she was preparing for her husband.

'I was home before six, and was just sitting down to my meal of meat and tea, when in came a well-dressed gentleman, and insisted on my setting off with him to marry his daughter. The company had all been waiting in anxious expectation, no minister appearing. There had been a mistake, and they had forgotten to send me notice, two having undertaken it. The bride was Widow Crockat, a nice-looking woman – you will remember her, Eliza; Mr. Taylor was the bridegroom. Famished, fatigued, bamboozled, I yet got through the ceremony quite safely, binding them hard and fast with all due solemnity. There were then some tears shed according to form, and then after-congratulations and wine. I was presented by the bridesmaid with a pair of long silk stockings, as large and massy as would serve a Bishop.

'I soon made my escape, and, after preparing and refreshing, met my people at seven – the families I had visited – in one house. There were three rooms full, and most of my audience were therefore out of sight: however, we

---

4. McCheyne's 'Old Light' friends might scarcely have approved of the term 'dissenters' which applies to them. From 1733 onwards they have preferred to be known as 'Seceders' – Christians in a state of compulsory Secession from the Kirk of Scotland, but ready to return so soon as it is 'free, faithful and reformed'.

5. 'Sowens' is Scots for a dish made from the farina remaining among the husks of oats.

are something like the Highlandman's gun that fired round
the corner. The people come well out, and seem to enjoy
it. One Roman Catholic, who heard me before, says, "Yon
minister beats a'; he maun be a Catholic".'

There were wider issues too, which began to enlist his
affection and to occupy part of his time. There was the cause
of Church Extension, for example. He became secretary in
Forfarshire of the association which sought the creation of
new parishes and the erection of additional places of worship. In October, 1837, he was one of a house-party at
Killermont, the residence of Mr. J. C. Colquhoun, who was
protagonist of the movement in Parliament. Dr. Chalmers
was there also, and the conversation, 'interesting and animating', was continued on two successive evenings to a late
hour. 'There was something holy,' the younger man felt,
'about the very atmosphere. Chalmers was sitting opposite
to me at this table, writing, his venerable countenance ex-
pressing peace and goodwill to men.' Out of this meeting
with the captain of whatever was worthiest and best in the
Scotland of the day – 'O good grey head which all men knew!
O voice from which their omens all men drew!' – came Mc-
Cheyne's active participation in the battle of Church Extension.

So he grew in personal character and in rich and fruitful
diligence. Behind it all, its source and its secret, was the life
which is hid with Christ in God. 'I have little courage, little
anything,' he wrote to Mr. Nairne of Dunsinnan; 'but I just
give my hand to Him as a little child does, and He leads me,
and I am happy; what do I desire more?' He would have
been at home in the Convention tent at Keswick, and he could
have sung the Keswick hymn:

> Stayed upon Jehovah,
>> Hearts are fully blest,
> Finding, as He promised,
>> Perfect peace and rest.

He lived in the attitude of trust and in the atmosphere of communion. But he took care to maintain the trust and to practise the communion. His first concern was the nurture of his own soul. Every morning he saw to it before he turned to anything else. He rose early that he might have time to spend with God. Probably he had gone to bed at a late hour of the night, jaded in body and in mind after a day of duty; but 'a soldier of the Cross,' he said, 'must endure hardness', and he was up betimes. He would sing a Psalm, to tune his spirit into harmony with heavenly things. Then he sat down to read, mark, learn, and inwardly digest the living Word of his Lord, often studying three chapters in succession. Then he gave himself to prayer, the effectual prayer which avails much. And he was more refreshed than if he had prolonged the hours of sleep; he was furnished and prepared for every good work. That his ideals of the good work were only heightened by his meditation in the secret place over the open Book, a quotation – very simple, very incisive, and very far-reaching – from one of those manuscript quartos into which we have glanced will bear testimony. It is headed: 'What should a minister be? Answered from 1 Thess. 2.'

And this is how the answer runs:

'1. *Bold in Our God*. Having the courage of one who is near and dear to God, and who has God dwelling in him.
2. *To speak the Gospel*. He should be a voice to speak the gospel, an angel of glad tidings.

3. *With much agony*. He should wrestle with God, and wrestle with men.

4. *Not of uncleanness*. He should be chaste in heart, in eye, in speech.

5. *Not of deceit or guile*. He should be open, having only one end in view, the glory of Christ.

6. *Allowed of God to be put in trust*. He should feel a steward, entrusted of God.

7. *Not as pleasing men, but God*. He should speak what God will approve, who tries the heart.

8. *Neither flattering words*. He should never flatter men, even to win them.

9. *Nor a cloke of covetousness*. Not seeking money or presents, devoted to his work with a single eye.

10. *Nor of men sought we glory*. Not seeking praise.

11. *Gentle even as a nurse*.

12. *Affectionately desirous of you*. Having an inward affection and desire for the salvation and growth of his people.

13. *Willing to impart our own souls*. Willing to suffer loss, even of life, in their cause.

14. *Laboriousness night and day*.

15. *To preach without being chargeable*, to any of his people.

16. *Holily*.

17. *Justly*.

18. *Unblameably we behaved among believers*. The daily walk.

19. *Exhorted every one*. Individuality of ministrations.

20. *As a father*. Authority and love.

21. *Thank we God*. He should be full of thanksgiving without ceasing.

22. Should be with his people *in heart, when not in presence*.

23. *Endeavoured to see you*.

24. *His people his hope*. That which animates him.

25. *And joy*. Immediate delight.

26. *And crown of rejoicing*. When he looks beyond the grave.'

There is something awesome, something active and sharper than a two-edged sword, in those deliberately numbered particulars.

One afternoon in 1838, when he was absent on Church Extension business in the company of Thomas Guthrie, then newly translated from Arbirlot to Edinburgh, the sister at home was startled by the contents of a letter he sent to her. 'My dear Eliza,' it said, 'you will be surprised that I do not come in with Mr. Guthrie. But I have had a tumble, and it is thought better that I remain here till to-morrow, when I propose to be in Dundee. Mr. G. will tell you how I got it. Tell James that there will be no class tonight; he must do his best to warn them not to come. I still hope to be at Blairgowrie on Wednesday; but, of course, I cannot be sure. Mr. and Mrs. Grierson are all kindness. No bones are broken; and I am only a little bruised, which pains my chest.' On the back of the letter the woman who received it, true-hearted and tender-hearted, has inscribed this: 'Robert, from Errol. *He keepeth all his bones; not one of them is broken.*' What had happened?

In the manse-garden at Errol stood some gymnastic poles which McCheyne himself had planned for the amusement of a boy-friend, the son of Mr. Grierson, minister of the beautiful village in the Carse of Gowrie. Boyish and sprightly himself, he challenged Mr. Guthrie to a trial of skill; but, when he was hanging by his heels and hands some six feet from the earth, one of the poles suddenly snapped, and, to the onlooker's horror, he came down on his back to the ground 'with a tremendous thud'. He sickened, and was carried into the manse. But God was keeping watch, and the results of the accident were less disastrous than they might have been; soon, to all appearance at least, its evil issues had passed.

Yet the flesh was weak.[6] Again and again he was reminded
of its frailty during those introductory years in Dundee. He
would not acknowledge defeat so long as it was possible to
fight on; there was a soldierly strain in him. 'My cough is

---

6. In Dr. Guthrie's Autobiography the consequences of this accident are
perhaps magnified overmuch. It is said to 'begin the illness that terminated in his death'; and it is added that he 'was never the same man
again'. But, through the kindness of Miss Bonar, I have before me a
letter written to her father, in August, 1874, by Dr. Grierson of Errol,
then an old man who had entered his eighty-fourth year. He recalls,
vividly enough, the incident of the long-past summer's forenoon.

'It happened on the 28th of August, 1838. Robert McCheyne had
been assisting at our Communion four weeks before; and, kindly amusing my elder boy, who had then entered his tenth year, by showing and
teaching him some athletic exercises, he suggested to me the erection of
a simple apparatus for this purpose. This was accomplished by the erection of two upright posts, about four feet asunder, one of them nailed to
a tree, and each of them perforated by a number of circular holes for
receiving the ends of a horizontal bar.

After breakfast Robert, delighted to find his recommendation attended to, proceeded to make use of the apparatus for himself, and asked
if it were strong enough. Thinking chiefly of the vertical pressure, I said
that a much heavier man than he had hung upon the horizontal bar, till
he raised his chin to be level with it.

Mr. McCheyne then instantly sprang upon it, and sat there at an el-
evation of nearly six feet from the ground. By a sudden lateral jerk, to
produce a somersault in descending, the leverage of his weight proved
to be too much for one of the uprights, which gave way by splitting at
one of the lower holes: thus causing the lamentable fall which Dr. Guthrie
has mentioned.

Medical assistance was immediately obtained; but no serious injury
had been received. After two days' rest he returned on his pony to Dundee, preached in his own church the following Sabbath, and next day
went on a visit to his friend, Mr. Macdonald at Blairgowrie... The utmost
that can be said as to the fall is, that it was justly regarded as an additional reason for his obtaining rest from hard study, pulpit, and other
professional labour.'

turned into a loose kind of grumble, like the falling down of a shower of stones in a quarry,' he assures his mother; 'and I am well and lively in all other respects.' She would have prescribed for him 'a gruel with white wine in it', but he knew a more efficacious remedy – 'I feel a great deal the better for preaching yesterday; it is the best cure for all slight colds'. His 'affectionate friend and leech', Dr. Gibson, was sometimes at his wits' end with a patient so valorous and so stubbornly reluctant to confess to any ailment; and once, after Eliza had been ill and was recovered, he seized the opportunity to read both of them a salutary lecture: 'She still must take the greatest care, and I do trust that in this one respect she will follow – and at the same time shew him – a much better example than her dear and reverend brother so incorrigibly sets her'. When he had to succumb, and to call in the physician, with what gaiety he recalled the episode as soon as it was over, and insisted on paying the fee!

> Dear Doctor, allow me to borrow a leaf
> From your book of prescriptions, commanding and brief,
> 'Hoc aurum et papyr.' Mix – pocket – call 'Dust'!
> And swallow it quickly. Come, Doctor, you must.
> I had sooner want stipend, want dinner, want tea,
> Than my doctor should ever work wanting his fee.
> Forgive this intrusion; and let me remain,
> In haste, your affectionate, R. M. McCheyne.
> *Dulce est desipere in loco.*

But, by the close of 1838, he was gravely ill, not so much through any lingering consequences of his fall, or through the old trouble in the lungs, as with a beating and palpitating heart which betokened general weakness and nerves unstrung. He was forced to leave Dundee for a time, and to return to the Edinburgh home. Week after week went by, and he was still there. Then, in the early spring of 1839, a totally unexpected prospect opened up in front of him; and many months elapsed before his congregation saw him again.

What a grief took possession of the people! Letter in succession to letter was sent to Edinburgh. One poor woman bewailed the loss of 'our golden candlestick, and bright star'. Three members signed their names to a pleading request for information about his health; 'when the heart is full,' they say, 'the lips must speak.' An office-bearer suggested that the absent minister should write a weekly pastoral letter to be read at the Thursday meeting; and this he often managed to do. A little private gathering of the elders, to which a few others joined themselves, was begun on the Monday evenings, with the express purpose of interceding for his recovery and of entreating God's blessing on the pastorless flock.

Andrew Bonar visited St. Peter's, and reported afterwards, 'You have left your sheep in the hand of the Good Shepherd. I heard the bleating of some of them, but the Lord will feed them.' He was sure, too, that McCheyne's retirement was part of God's plan, and that its harvest would be as beneficent as that of his tasking and toiling had been. 'I have been thinking that in our day there is such need of the Spirit that it would not be surprising if God were to lead those of His servants who *will* pray into *a desert place apart*, taking Elijah from the thousands of Israel, to whom he might have testified, in order to watch solitary on Carmel and pray seven times for the coming rain.' It was a word spoken in season, and a true forecast of the Day of the Lord at hand.

CHAPTER 5

Those Holy Fields

One of McCheyne's sermons, preserved in the *Memoir and Remains*, is on the Pauline text, *To the Jew first*. It dates from the November of 1839. But it had a predecessor, nearly two years older, whose arguments and illustrations may be read in one of the manuscript volumes that hold in condensed and attenuated form so many of his discourses. Why, he asks, should the gospel be preached in the first instance to the sons and daughters of Israel? Four reasons are assigned.

There is the commandment of God; and Old Testament and New are quoted to prove how distinct and decisive is the divine will in the matter.

There are His promises to the friends of His ancient people, His threatenings against their foes.

There is His love of them even in their captivity, an undying love which earnestly remembers them still.

And, once again, there is their importance to the life and health of the world: to its waste lands and its thirsty citizens a regenerated Israel will be *as a dew from the Lord*.

Thus early in his ministry, McCheyne made disclosure of that warmth of affection which throbbed within him for the Jew.

And now he was to see Palestine for himself. It was a marvel of which he had not dreamed when he left Dundee in his invalided condition. But the illness seemed to some of his friends one main cause why he should go; the journey, it was thought, with its change of scenery and occupation might put vigour into his feeble frame. A short time before this, the Church of Scotland, with that fresh-born anxiety which was stirring within it for the progress of Christ's kingdom, had determined to send to the Holy Land, and to the countries of Eastern and Central Europe, a Mission of Inquiry into the state of the Jews – their numbers, condition, and character.

Two veterans had been selected, of whose 'learning, piety, zeal and prudence' the General Assembly was fully satisfied – Dr. Alexander Keith, minister of St. Cyrus, and author of various books on the subject of Prophecy, and Dr. Alexander Black, Professor of Theology in Marischal College, Aberdeen.

With them was joined a much-respected elder of the West, Mr. Robert Wodrow of Glasgow: he was great-grandson of the penman of the *Analecta*. Surely it was a thousand pities that in the end of the day Mr. Wodrow found himself prevented from sharing in the enterprise; for the idea of it had really originated with him, and had been for years a fondly-cherished dream.

But now it was proposed, Dr. Candlish being chiefly responsible for the suggestion, that Robert McCheyne and Andrew Bonar should form part of the deputation. 'See the kindness of your Heavenly Physician!' the latter writes to the former on the 8th of March, 1839 – 'His cure for you is *the fragrance of Lebanon* and the balmy air of *Thy land, O Immanuel*'.

For a while, however, Mr. Bonar was uncertain as to his own duty. 'Your way is clear,' he says in the same letter. 'I rejoice for the consolation it must give you, under your sore trial of silence, to see that your feet may carry the message of peace in another way than formerly. But is my way so clear? I do not feel that I can yet sing the song which I have put into your lips –

> God is the Lord Who unto us
> Hath made light to arise.

'My difficulties are:

'1. Since you have Dr. Black with you, you have little need of me in regard to languages.

'2. Your argument, drawn from the importance of the subject, is in this manner turned aside from its reference to me; for all the object of the tour may be obtained by the three worthy and gifted men that form the deputation, even though the fourth remain in the fields of Ephratah.

'3. I have got no light whatsoever as to supply for my parish; on the contrary, I cannot ascertain, though I have made inquiry, whether or no the appointment would be left to me. Now, to leave my people in this state seems to me like a shepherd, whose voice his own sheep know, calling the flock into a field, and then all at once leaving them to the danger of grieving wolves. The very circumstance that as yet I do not know of conversions among them seems to me a reason for not going; they being just now in some degree, to human appearance, like Edwards's people the year before the work began, full of attention, and outwardly improved, and the young uncommonly willing to take advice.'

Andrew Bonar, like the apostle who wrote to the Philippians, was *in a strait betwixt two*; but at last all the hindrances obstructing his path were removed. 'The great cause of Israel,' he saw, 'would perhaps be benefited' if he shared in the Mission. And as for his parishioners in Collace, on the eve apparently of a year of the grace of God – 'I will not fear to trust the Lord with the souls of my people; when John the Baptist was removed, Christ Himself came'.

It was certainly a happy arrangement for McCheyne that this friend of his heart was to be beside him. The two older men, as it turned out, were compelled to abandon the heats and toils of Syria in advance of their associates; and then David and Jonathan could stay behind, to prosecute to its termination the sacred work which had led them so far from their Scottish homes, and in which they both had so unalloyed a delight.

St. Peter's sent McCheyne its benediction. 'In agreeing to the proposal,' the elders wrote on the 11th of March, 'we know well that you have been actuated by a sense of duty; and, even if it had not been urged upon you by considerations affecting your own health, in which your people feel an anxious concern, we would have been reluctant to raise any obstacle in the way of a plan fraught with consequences so deeply interesting not merely to the house of Israel, but to the Church of Christ.

'Though separated from one another for a season,' they continue, 'we shall have the privilege of meeting at a Throne of Grace, and of bearing our mutual anxieties and desires to the footstool of that Throne. There we shall often think of our absent minister. There, we know well, his people will not be forgotten by him.'

Thus the long, farewell letter, eloquent all through of the tender intimacies uniting the teacher and the taught, and demonstrating in every sentence the wisdom and the goodness of the men who drew it up, passes on to its beautiful conclusion.

'May God be the Companion of your journey. May He refresh your soul by rich communications of His love. May

He conduct you in safety to the place of your destination. And when your feet stand amidst the ruins of the once-glorious Temple, on that Mount Zion which was *beautiful for situation, the joy of the whole earth*, may the Spirit Himself come down upon you *as the dew of Hermon, the dew that descended upon the mountains of Zion*. There may the Lord *command the blessing, even life for evermore*. Again, we commend you to the keeping of the God of Abraham and of Isaac and of Jacob.'

The congregation was thrice and four times fortunate which had such a minister and such office-bearers.

There is no need to linger over the details of a journey which, at the time it was undertaken, was a rare and singular achievement. 'We are not aware,' say the authors of the *Narrative of a Mission of Inquiry to the Jews*, 'that any clergyman of the Church of Scotland was ever privileged to visit the Holy City before; and now that four of us had been brought thus far by the good hand of our God upon us, we trusted that it might be a token for good, and perhaps the dawn of a brighter day on our beloved church – a day of generous self-denied exertion in behalf of scattered Israel and a perishing world.' The story is told in full in this *Narrative*, which Andrew Bonar and Robert McCheyne put together after their return; of which Dr. Chalmers wrote to one of them, 'I have the greatest value for it'; and which makes a book well worth reading to this hour, because of the light which it throws on Scripture, and because of that fervour of love which palpitates through its chapters for the seed of Abraham, God's children who are 'long lost but longer dear'.

But here are the letters, minute, careful, vivid, which McCheyne sent home – fifteen letters in all. They trace his itinerary from Hampstead, on the 29th of March, 1839, through France and Italy, Valetta, Alexandria, the quarantine camp at the foot of Carmel, Beyrout and Smyrna, Galatz and Tarnopol and Breslau, back to the Thames on the 6th of November. We may glance through their closely-packed pages, in search of what illuminates the man himself rather than for the information they give of the scenes he saw and the people he met.

How instinctively, 'as the sunflower ever turning to the mighty sun', his thought and heart were accustomed to lift themselves to God and the better world, the very first of them makes evident. On the voyage between Edinburgh and London, he noticed the sea-gulls following the boat, not straight, but flying hither and thither: 'so my soul follows Christ, not as I would desire, for then I should never wander from Him, but hither and thither, faint yet pursuing'. He heard the captain say, when someone asked if the wind were fair, 'Quite fair, but not enough to make sail'; and 'many Christians,' he reflected, 'seem to have God's Spirit fair enough, but not sufficiently strong to make sail; they do not go forward.' Off Cromer Point he saw the regularly recurring flash of the lighthouse: 'so may God's ministers be a beacon on the waters, guiding those who sail in a calm sea and those who are near shipwreck; like this, too, may they revolve, shedding benediction on all within the range of their influence.'

The wilderness of London appalled him: 'this city wears away all my thoughts and feelings'. But we are pleased to discover that the bow, now and then, could be unbent; with his hostess he visited the Coliseum, to witness 'a truly wonderful panorama' of the metropolis; 'my head felt quite giddy, and I feared to look over lest I shall fall from the top of St. Paul's'.

Landed in France, he found a hundred novelties to kindle

attention and interest. There was a dinner, more astonishing than satisfying, in the inn at Abbeville; 'there were so many things that I was like to be starved, and harpers entertaining us all the while: this is something like Solomon's experience in Ecclesiastes'. 'Poor Paris,' he mourned, 'knows no Sabbath.' Driving away in the diligence from Bar-sur-Aube, he and his friends busied themselves all day long in scattering leaflets from the windows of the vehicle, among the passersby and in the village streets; 'first it began with the youthful members of the Deputation, but soon the contagion spread, till we had the delightful sight of a Professor of Theology handing out tracts or flinging them on the wings of the wind to those in the fields, crying, "Voilà! Un petit livre pour votre enfant!" '

It was a relief when the lumbering and wearisome prison of the diligence was exchanged for the freedom of the riverboat on the Saône or the Rhone; at Avignon, he tells his sister, 'the arrowy Rhone is a splendid stream, broad, deep, and rapid; and the whole sail down it is one of the grandest in the world'. But at the river's mouth they were met by the violence of the mistral, blowing in from the Mediterranean; and in the storm the Frenchmen were little else than blunderers – 'it was really amusing, if it had not been dangerous, to see how they ran about, one for the anchor, another for the cable, another to the helm: all was confusion'.

That Sabbath, the Sacrament Day in St. Peter's, was spent, perforce, on a small and lonely island; 'about a dozen of fishermen's cabins, with a fig-tree in the garden and a vine over the door, a herd of asses, and a waste of rushes, formed the scenery of the place; we sat under a bush, and read the account of Paul's shipwreck at Melita, and on the whole had a quiet and delightful Sabbath'.

Then came 'the glorious bay of Genoa'; and afterwards there was a week among the synagogues and Rabbis of Leghorn, where much excitement was awakened by the Scottish missionaries and their errand. In the *Lycurgus*, 'a very splendid steamer and ship of war', the voyage was made from Leghorn to Malta; and 'I felt it sweet,' McCheyne says, 'to lie and see the sea round and round, a complete circle to the horizon on all sides; it made me feel so little and God so great.'

Between Valetta and Alexandria he 'began to think of Major Donald's story of the Highland sergeant in the West Indies, saluting his officer every morning with "Anither het day, your Honour!" – it is too true in these latitudes'; but among the isles of Greece Andrew Bonar and he forgot such trivial inconveniences, and quoted Homer to each other, and 'gazed and gazed between Icaria and Naxos to see if the eye could reach Patmos, where John was so highly favoured of God'.

And the commotion of the landing in Alexandria – 'you cannot imagine! It baffles all description: boys with donkeys, men with camels, wild-looking porters, Greeks and Turks, all roaring in sonorous Arabic, all eager to be at ourselves and our luggage. By help of Mr. Waghorn's agent, who laid about him with his stick, we got our luggage on human backs and ourselves on donkeys; and away we went full gallop through the narrow streets. Women with their faces covered all but the eyes, women carrying their little children astride on the shoulders, fakirs, soldiers, children, all had to rush out of our way; and many a contemplative Turk took his hookah from his mouth, to see what strange figures hurried by.' Robert McCheyne was drinking his first draught of the fascination of the East.

Preparations followed for the march through the Desert – the purchase of carpets and quilts, 'nice pillows also which

Jacob had not when he slept at Bethel'; the hire of donkeys, tents, and drivers; the securing of the two servants – Ibrahim, 'a handsome, small-made Egyptian', and Achmet the cook, 'a dark good-natured fellow with a white turban and bare dark legs'. So the pilgrims set forward; and 'you will be anxious, my dear Mamma, but you must just be still, and know that God is God'. They had their fatigues, their hardships, their dangers, the most serious and alarming of the mishaps being the fall of Dr. Black from his camel; but they were brought safely through, and in the end were 'in fully better condition' than when they began. As for the writer himself, 'you must not imagine that I have altogether lost the palpitation of my heart, for it often visits me to humble and prove me; and still its visits are not nearly so frequent'. Among the mounds of Zoan they made their own discoveries, of pottery and vitrified stones, of two sphinxes and many obelisks.

Entering the country of the Philistines, McCheyne was impressed by its likeness and yet its unlikeness to what it had been once. 'This is the way up out of Egypt, little changed from the day that Joseph and Mary carried down the Babe from the anger of Herod. Little changed, did I say? It is all changed! The River of Egypt, Wady Gaza, Eshcol, Sorek, every brook we crossed was dried up, not a drop of water. The land is changed; it is rich no more; the sand struggles with the grass for mastery. The cities are changed; where are they? The people are changed; no more the bold Philistines, no more the children of Simeon, no more Isaac and his herdmen, no more David and his horsemen; but miserable Arab shepherds, simple people without ideas, poor, degraded, fearful.'

On the 7th of June, 'one of the most privileged days of our life', he had his first view of Jerusalem. 'I left my camel and went before, hurrying over the burning rocks. In about half an hour Jerusalem came in sight. How doth the city sit solitary, that was full of people! Is this the perfection of beauty? How hath the Lord covered the daughter of Zion with a cloud in His anger! It is indeed very desolate. Read the two first chapters of Lamentations, and you have a vivid picture of what we saw.'

In and out of the marvellous town they went during the next ten days, making excursions from their lodgings on Olivet to Bethany and Bethlehem and Hebron; and then the rapid increase of the plague in the crowded streets and in-sanitary houses led them to turn their faces northward.

For more than a week they were encamped at the foot of Carmel, on the edge of the blue waters of the Mediterra-nean. 'I plucked a rose of Sharon for you,' he told Eliza in his next letter, 'and concealed it under my saddle. But alas! it dropped. I am of opinion that the rose of Sharon is the splendid rhododendron, which blooms there in magnificent profusion. It is like Christ, altogether lovely.'

A little later, at Beyrout, the pleasant companionship had to be broken up. 'Our venerable fellow-traveller, Dr. Black,' McCheyne explained, 'has for some time felt the heat of Syria and the mode of travelling too much for him. He and Dr. Keith have accordingly resolved on returning by the Dan-ube. We felt sorry indeed to part.'

The two younger men were left alone, but in God's kind and watchful providence a new ally was given them. In Beyrout they found a Christian Jew, whom they had met as they passed through London, Erasmus Calman, a man who knew Palestine from Dan to Beersheba, and who was famil-iar with Arabic, Polish, and German, as well as with Eng-lish; 'so that,' as McCheyne said, 'we shall be better off than ever in regard to making inquiries.'

They went south again, and other goodbyes were spoken – to Ibrahim and Achmet, 'with tears on both sides'; they had two Roman Catholic servants now, and two muleteers, the one a Maronite and the other a Druse: many shades of religious belief were represented in the little cavalcade. Having seen Sidon and the ruins of Tyre, they wheeled round to the east, to make the acquaintance with Safed and the Sea of Galilee and Mount Tabor and Nazareth. By and by, they were back in Beyrout, waiting for the steamer which should carry them to Smyrna.

But, at this point in their wanderings, it appeared as if Robert McCheyne were to start on a supremer journey, to the Throne of God, to which we are led by her whom the old Earl of Manchester named 'Death the mother of Life', and not Marah but Naomi – 'O sweet word, Life, the best monosyllable in the world!' What the origin of his illness was he could scarcely tell, unless it might be that he had caught fever from a young Glasgow lad, whom he visited in the hospital, and on whose hot brow he had laid his own hand. The doctor who was called to see him had him sent a thousand feet up the mountain-side, out of the stifling air of Beyrout; and here, in a few days, he mended so much that it seemed the wisest plan to set sail for Smyrna without further delay.

At first, the cool sea-breezes had a reviving effect; and by sunset, though he was very weak, he found himself talking with some Jews, whom he encountered now for the fourth time, and who were grieved indeed to see him laid low. But the night was sleepless, and in the morning, when they anchored for some hours off Cyprus, he was in high fever. 'They helped me on deck under the awning; but I felt as I never felt before. I knew I had a Father in heaven who had forgiven and redeemed me, and therefore I resolved to fear no evil. My voice became very low, almost inaudible. I thought my head would burst in two. At last, my faculties one by one began to give way. I could not remember where we were going. Still, I thought of you all, and, although I could not expect ever to see you again, I prayed that my death might be more blessed to you than all my life had been.'

But, when leeches had been got from Cyprus, which the steward applied to the back of the sick man's head, there was some improvement; and so things continued, now a little better and then unmistakably worse, until at length, to the sufferer's thankfulness, Smyrna was reached.

There, however, the inn was dismal, the walls so thin that the place would be like an oven when the sun was up, the rooms small, the noise of the sailors and pedestrians and traffickers in the streets dreadful. Happily, Salvo, the innkeeper, had a kindly heart; he owned another hostelry, he said, an hour's ride into the country, at a village called Bouja; could the stranger venture so far? To all concerned it seemed the best course, and Salvo himself accompanied them, and McCheyne's donkey-driver lent him a helping hand at the steep parts of the road, and the promise of the 91st Psalm was fulfilled, *He shall give His angels charge over thee.*

At Bouja it was more than ever manifest that God had been keeping guard. For, first, the officers of a man-of-war lying in Smyrna roads had ridden out to the village that day on a little excursion, the doctor being one of their number; and he understood immediately the gravity of the case, and busied himself in ministering to the patient. And, next, there were the Anglican chaplain and his wife, Mr. and Mrs. Lewis, 'both delightful Christians', who had a house in Bouja; and, after one night had been spent in the inn, he had the invalid carried on a sofa to the shelter of his own roof, and for three weeks she watched over him as his own mother would have done; until at last, eight days after Andrew Bonar and Erasmus Calman had left Smyrna for Constantinople, he was allowed to follow.

'Do lay all this to heart' – so he sums up the story of distress and deliverance; 'you see how easily I might have been gone, and how God has spared me to you. O, that you may be drawn by His mercies to take Him for a Father, as He is to all who are washed in the blood of His Son!' As for himself, he never forgot the tendernesses, of earth and heaven, which had been lavished on his head.

> Bouja, farewell! Blest be the Hand
> That led me to thy calm retreat,

he sang in his gratitude.

> Thy cypresses of deepest green
>   I'll long in vain to see;
> Thy fragrant flowering jessamine,
>   So often plucked for me.

Two months and a half of travel remained to him before he was back in Scotland. They were occupied in visiting the chief centres of Jewish population in Moldavia, Roumania, and Austrian and Prussian Poland.

On the Danube, he 'sometimes thinks of the gladiator's rude hut, and sees plenty of Dacian mothers and young barbarians all at play'.

At Galatz, to his intense joy, the English consul turns out to be an old High School boy, Charles Cunningham; 'we took great delight in recalling past scenes in which we shared;

we felt like birds escaped from our cage, when, after being examined by the Doctor, we were let go'.

In Bucharest he buys 'a cloak of fox-skin, which keeps me quite warm night and day', while his friends and he are being hurried from stage to stage over rough roads that seem to have no ending.

One night, at Jassy, he is present at a Jewish wedding, and, knowing that Eliza will ask him what manner of dress the bride had on, he 'subjoins a facsimile'; 'you see what a lesson of modesty the covered faces teach our Scottish brides'.

Austria looks to him the most bigoted and suspicious of all lands; at the Custom House in Brody, 'my desk afforded the officials matter for deep inquiry, there being sketches and plans and a handwriting not a little mysterious; the map of my parish arrested their attention, and I thought we should all have been imprisoned for it, for one maintained that it was something Russian, and they are very jealous of that'.

Outside a Galician village he has a narrow escape from injury at the hands of two evil-minded shepherds. 'They made signs that I should go with them. I refused. They showed that I must. I persisted in my way. When they threw themselves in my path, I pushed them aside and ran. I could easily have outstripped them, but did not like to make my heart beat, as a hard race would have done. I therefore stopped, and with my trusty staff stood on the defensive. I could not find it in my heart to strike them, and so they soon closed upon me, and we had a wrestle together, in which my coat was torn from top to bottom. I sat down tired on the ground, when they, for what reason I know not, left me, and I proceeded quietly home. I was afterwards told that they wanted to rob me, and that they would not have scrupled in the least to use the knife. It is only another instance in which God has wonderfully preserved me. Surely I should live to praise Him.'

But there are pleasanter incidents to picture to the home-friends. In Cracow, to the English-speaking missionary labouring among the Jews and to the missionary's wife, as well as to his own companions in travel, he dispenses the Sacrament of the Lord's Supper; 'it was sweet to cling together in that holy ordinance in so dark and dead a spot'. And at the very end of the eventful journey, when they are in Hamburg, he preaches 'for the first time since leaving England, and feels nothing the worse for it'. Is it not a pledge that it may be the Father's will to restore him to usefulness again among his beloved flock?

McCheyne's soul was more than ever revealed to himself and to others by the experiences of this memorable year. One thing which they rendered evident was the wideness of his sympathy and aspiration. It has been hinted already that in his student days he had coveted the life of a Foreign Missionary. That was not to be, his own uncertain health, and God's wiser guidance of his footsteps alike forbidding it. But the mission to the Jews disclosed and deepened the old longing; it showed that his Christianity was as far removed as it could be from everything parochial or sectional or partial; it drew out his affections and his prayers in fuller measure to other lands and peoples than his own. Especially, of course, it was the illustration of his sense of indebtedness to Israel, and of his hunger to repay the heavy and age-long debt. There was nothing perfunctory or professional in his manner of fulfilling the trust which the General Assembly had confided to him. All through, it was a love-darg; and the love was of that sovereign sort which many waters could not quench, and the coals of which burned with a most vehement flame.

Thus he began, on board the boat between Granton pier
and London docks, in earnest talk with a young recreant Jew,
a Mr. Tobias, 'gentlemanly, showy, and luxurious', who kept
his Tephilloth and Torah – his Prayer Book and Book of the
Law – at the bottom of his portmanteau; to whom he read in
Hebrew the first Psalm, and whom he implored to meditate
in God's law day and night. Thus he continued, nowhere miss-
ing an opportunity of visiting a synagogue or of discussion
with a Rabbi, staying in a Jewish khan wherever that was
practicable, and as often as he could engaging a Jewish driver
to carry him across the great spaces of Eastern and Central
Europe. And thus he ended, in 'much interesting converse'
in Hamburg with Mr. Moritz, the Christian missionary to
the children of Abraham.

Every page of every letter he sent home demonstrated his
quenchless desire for the salvation of God's ancient people;
and, once he was in Scotland again, he strove, in season and
out of season, to bring the Church into agreement with his
own passion and enthusiasm. That, since 1839, she has done
something for the ingathering of the lost sheep of the house
of Israel is due in large degree to the *Wanderjahr* of Robert
Murray McCheyne.[1]

---

1. In 1841 the Rev. Daniel Edward was ordained as the first missionary
of the Church of Scotland to the Jews. His ministry was exercised in
Jassy, Lemberg, and Breslau – a ministry of rich spiritual power, prolonged through fifty-four years. Long and interesting letters survive,
which were written by Mr. Edward to McCheyne.

The Budapest Mission dates from the following year, 1842. Dr. Keith
and Dr. Black had come home through Hungary from Palestine. In Budapest Dr. Keith was for a time dangerously ill, and was nursed by Maria
Dorothea, the Princess Palatine of Hungary, a lady who was a Protestant
and a saint. Out of her interest in the Scottish ministers a great work of
evangelization has sprung. 'Rabbi' Duncan was one of the first mission-

But if the circumference of his sympathies was wide, his thoughts and intercessions had a centre to which they gravitated continually back. Absence from Dundee and from St. Peter's only tightened those bonds which God Himself had bound.

On the Rhone he writes, 'My heart is much with my dear people'.

In Beyrout these are his hopes and his confessions, 'Perhaps my Great Master will fully recover me, and I shall preach among them once more the unsearchable riches of Christ. I sometimes think I set my heart too much upon this; and that God has sent me away to teach me He can save and feed them without any help of mine, and that His will, not my will, must be done.'

From Tarnopol he is drawn affectionately towards them,

---

aries to Budapest; and Dr. Adolph Saphir and Dr. Alfred Edersheim were among the early converts of the Mission. Over its schools and preaching-halls and many agencies for good, Dr. Andrew Moody presided for forty years; and Mr. James Webster is a successor worthy of those who have gone before him. The most recent, and one of the most informative and delightful, accounts of the Budapest Mission will be found in *La Hongrie Calviniste*, by Professor Doumergue, of the University of Montauban (Toulouse, 1912, pp. 52-56). Professor Doumergue says: 'La Mission chez les Juifs apporta des idées, des modèles, des excitations, et elle fut comme un foyer lumineux et chaud, au sein du protestantisme hongrois'.

It was not until the eighties of the last century that McCheyne's prayer that his Church should establish Mission-stations within the borders of Palestine itself was answered. In the *Narrative* he and Andrew Bonar write: 'Thus our last evening in Safed came to a close. We could not help desiring that the time would come when our beloved Church would be permitted to establish a Mission here .... The headquarters might be at Safed in summer and at Tiberias in winter.' Today the United Free Church has its missionaries, both men and women – preachers, doctors, nurses, and teachers – in Tiberias, in Safed, and in Hebron.

as Paul was to the Thessalonian disciples from Corinth: 'Dear
people,' he cries, 'my heart yearns over them at a distance';
in his relation to them he was *as gentle as a mother is when
she tenderly nurses her own children.*

Again, at the lakeside of Tiberias, he is pulled in two di-
rections, and Scotland haunts memory and spirit though Palestine is before the eyes.

> How pleasant to me thy deep blue wave,
>   O Sea of Galilee!
> For the glorious One Who came to save
>   Hath often stood by thee.
>
> Fair are the lakes in the land I love,
>   Where pine and heather grow;
> But thou hast loveliness far above
>   What nature can bestow.

Capernaum speaks its solemn message to the town, thousands of miles distant, beside the Tay.

> Tell me, ye mouldering fragments, tell,
>   Was Christ's Own city here?
> Lifted to heaven, has it sunk to hell,
>   With none to shed a tear?
>
> Ah, would that my flock from thee might learn
>   How days of grace will flee!
> How all from an offered Christ that turn
>   Shall mourn at last like thee!

And Galilee sounds a summons in his own ears.

> And was it beside this very Sea
> >The Saviour three times said? –
> 'Simon Barjona, lovest thou Me?
> >My lambs and sheep then feed.'
>
> Saviour, ascended to God's right hand,
> >Yet the same Saviour still,
> Graved on my heart is this lovely strand
> >And every fragrant hill.
>
> O give me, Lord, by this sacred wave,
> >Threefold Thy love divine,
> That I may feed, till I find my grave,
> >Thy flock, both Thine and mine! [2]

With such wishes, such prayers, and such loves mastering him, his heart leaped up when, at Hamburg, the news came that the powers of Pentecost were being manifested once more in his native land. 'We have heard something of a reviving work at Kilsyth,' he writes to his father and mother, as he sailed in the *Lady Lonsdale* up the Thames. 'We saw it noticed in one of the newspapers. I also saw the name of Dundee associated with it; so that I earnestly hope good has been doing in our Church, and the dew from on high watering our parishes, and that the flocks whose pastors have been wandering may have shared in the blessing. We are quite ignorant of the facts, and you may believe are very anxious to hear.'

In a few days the anxiety was to be exchanged for an amazement and a joy, which filled his mouth with laughter and his tongue with singing.

---

2. Where the wording of these lines differs from the customary version, McCheyne's pencilled copy in his travel-notebook has been followed.

CHAPTER 6

Then Drops From Heaven Fell

One burden had lain on McCheyne's heart as he looked forward to his journeying. It was the thought of the congregation he must leave behind. Up in the Heavenlies, he was confident, the Chief Shepherd would be mindful of its necessity; but there must be a human shepherd close at hand to care for the flock. Where was this true man to be found?

Alexander Somerville helped the anxious minister to the solution of the question. Writing on the 1st of March, 1839, to his 'dear Robert', he reported: 'I delivered your message to Burns, who liked the idea very much of taking your place for a season, but of course could not say whether it would be in his power to do so or not. He is in the hands of the Colonial Committee; and it is probable he will go either to America or to Ceylon. He will know immediately, however, what is to be done with him, and will then return an answer to your letter himself.'

The difficulties which Alexander Somerville foresaw were soon removed. Neither India nor New Brunswick was to be William Burns's destination; and by the 11th of the month he could tell McCheyne that he was free to give himself to Dundee. A week before he had laid bare his soul in characteristic phraseology to the man who was eager for his aid. 'I am indeed unfit, as I am unworthy, to engage in this arduous but most noble embassage. I am darkness; I am deadness; I am carnal, sold under sin. But what then? Glory be to Jesus, His grace is sufficient for *me*; for His strength is made perfect in weakness.' Plainly, this was no hireling, but a good shepherd, who would feed the little lambs and tend well the sheep.

In the muster-roll of the saints, William Chalmers Burns stands in the same high and princely rank with Robert Murray McCheyne. His is a life-story which divides itself into two strangely contrasted parts: the crowded years, first, of revival work in Britain and in Canada, when he spoke to vast multitudes, and when one stirring and rapturous excitement followed hard upon another; and then the years, as glorious in reality, of patient waiting and plodding pioneer toil in China, when the good seed was sown in simple and indomitable faith, but when the sheaves did not appear.

Yet the man was woven of one piece throughout. Always his earnestness was incandescent. Always his courage was devoid of fear and ignorant of the meaning of the word. Always the sight of the multitudes moved him to compassion. Always he was unworldly, and what most of us would reckon an impossible sacrifice was no sacrifice at all in his estimate of things. Always he distrusted himself, and had no honour and no friend but Christ, and lived only to blazon abroad the sufficiency of the Lamb of God and the Saviour of souls.

'The longing of my heart,' he said, 'would be to go once all round the world before I die, and preach one gospel invitation in the ear of every creature.' The last words which an early friend ever heard from him, standing one night under cold November skies at his father's door in Kilsyth, were, 'We must run!'; and to the end his feet were shod with the sandals of alacrity and self-crucifying love. 'We must not study comfort,' he told the mate of a trading vessel whom he met in Niewchang a month or two before death came; 'they that go to the front of the battle get the blessing; the skulkers

get no blessing'. There was never a thought of skulking in
his mind. His mother likened him to a knife that would be
worn out by cutting, not by rusting; and he 'wished it might
be so'.

And, wherever he went, the apostolic antithesis held good
of him, *As having nothing and yet possessing all things*. 'How
vividly do I remember the moment, a little more than a year
ago,' writes his brother and biographer, 'when the trunk which
had come home from China, containing nearly all of the prop-
erty that he left behind him in the world, was opened amid a
group of young and wondering faces! There were a few sheets
of Chinese printed matter, a Chinese and an English Bible,
an old writing-case, one or two small books, a Chinese lan-
tern, a single Chinese dress, and the blue flag of "the Gospel
boat!". "Surely," whispered a little one amid the awe-struck
silence, "surely he must have been *very* poor!" ' It was absolutely true, and as absolutely false. Since Christ was his, and
since Christ deigned to use him, he counted himself rich
beyond the dreams of avarice.

'To be in union with Him who is the Shepherd of Israel,'
he maintained, 'and to walk very near to Him who is a Sun
and Shield – that comprehends all that a poor sinner requires
to make him happy between this and heaven.' His delight in
Christ could not be hidden. It revealed itself in everything –
in the signature of his letters, for example. Sometimes it was,
'Yours in the Beloved'; or sometimes 'Wishing you conformity
to the Son of God, yours always'; or sometimes, 'Yours in
haste, with the affectionate desires of a cold heart'; and again,
'Yours in Emmanuel'; and yet again, 'Yours ever in Jesus
Our Hope'. The Presbytery of Aberdeen, wise and prudent,
took him to task for these exuberant signatures, but, while
he admitted that there was a risk of the pen outrunning the

soul, he protested too that no language more conventional and less tremblingly awake could ever satisfy him. Nor could it. He belonged to his Lord and Saviour Jesus Christ without any reserves. 'Know him, sir?' exclaimed a brother-mission-ary, 'all China knows him; he is the holiest man alive.'

Such was McCheyne's substitute in Dundee. He came to St. Peter's a young licentiate of twenty-four. Between him and the preacher whose place he was taking, the resemblances and the contrasts were both conspicuous.

They were alike in education and culture,[1] in the endow-ment of a Christianity which possessed and ruled the whole man, in an absorbing desire to win their hearers for their Master, in the baptism and unction of the Spirit of God.

But in temperament, in speech, and in methods of work they were widely separated.

McCheyne was physically frail; Burns had a bodily vig-our that seemed tireless and unconquerable: the one left the pulpit with a fluttering and agitated heart, while the other slept soundly, like a little child, after the most exhausting day of labour, and rose in the morning fresh and joyful as a strong man to run again his race.

McCheyne had fancy and pathos and beauty of utterance, even if he had cracked and marred that musical voice of his with overmuch speaking; Burns had a voice of splendid com-pass which could command any audience however great, indoors or out under the canopy of the sky, but he could not lay claim to the poetic diction of his friend or to his accents of gentle insistence – he was clear as a diamond, forcible and compelling, always direct and urgent, often blunt and bald, but often dramatic and unforgettable; when in his addresses

---

1. In the revival at Kilsyth, William Burns would relieve the tension of his mind by reading the Greek classics.

he 'bloomed fables' they resembled those of 'grand rough old Martin Luther' – they were 'flowers on furze', and probably 'the better the uncouther': they stuck, they clung, they made the listeners restless and ill at ease.

McCheyne was equable in his public work, and seldom lost the sense of accomplishing something for eternity; Burns was much more subjective, and on occasion had no liberty at all: at Moulin, for instance – 'I was so dark and dead that I had to draw quickly to a close, and I told Mr. Campbell that I could not speak at that time for the whole world'; and yet, after the benediction had been pronounced, and no one had gone away, and prayer had been offered up, 'throwing down the gauntlet to the enemies of Jesus, I spoke for a long time with such assistance that I felt as if I could have shaken the globe to pieces, through the views I got of the glory of the divine person of Christ and of His atoning sacrifice to rescue sinners from eternal death; the people were bent down beneath the Word like corn under the breeze, and many a stout sinner wept bitterly'.

From McCheyne the river of God flowed forth, healing, cooling, refreshing, usually quiet and tranquil in its progress; from Burns the mighty rushing wind of the Lord emanated and pealed, driving out death before its tempestuous onset, and by its extraordinary energy creating an immediate and victorious life; to him one may apply the words which a singer of today has used of William Booth –

> His voice
> Was like the sea-wind; when it blew abroad,
> Men's souls, in the salt wilderness astray,
> Deafened and blind with their own sound and spray,
> Came multitudinous rolling in to God.[2]

---

2. Mr. James Rhoades, in the *Westminster Gazette*.

There are diversities of gifts; but, where the consecration is so humble and so complete, there is the same Spirit. Both for McCheyne and for Burns that significant story is apposite which is narrated of the latter: how, in Blair Atholl an old Highland woman returned day after day to listen to his preaching, sitting on the pulpit stair and drinking in every syllable, though English was an unknown and foreign tongue to her. 'What was the use of her hearing him?' she was asked, and 'O,' she replied, 'I can understand the Holy Ghost's English!' The two spokesmen in St. Peter's Church were familiar with the Holy Ghost's English; they employed no other dialect; and, to their undying health and joy, thousands understood them.

When he assumed the care of the congregation in April, 1839, William Burns found himself in a field sown and watered, where the green blade was already springing up. This was no fallow ground that required to be broken and prepared. The issues of Robert McCheyne's unremitting work and perpetual prayer were now to become manifest; the proof was to be furnished that his labours and intercessions had not been in vain. We think it strange that another should step in to reap the sheaves; although our Lord has admonished us that frequently this is the celestial Husbandman's ordinance and law; and we have heard McCheyne himself, far away in Beyrout, confess his feeling that perhaps he had been sent to the distant land, for the express purpose of learning how God could save and bless his people without him.

But let us remember all the planning and toiling, the pleading and the weeping, which had preceded *the beginning of barley harvest* in our Scottish Bethlehem, House of the Bread of Life; and we shall see that McCheyne, no less than his successor, had part and lot in the happy ingathering. Burns was quick to recognize and to honour the service which had been so faithfully and so fruitfully performed. 'When I came among your people,' he wrote, 'I found such evidences of the Lord's work, in convincing and converting sinners, as was truly refreshing to my soul, after having spent more than seven years from the time when, if ever, I was brought to know the Lord, without alas! seeing so much as a single case of open and visible transition, from darkness to light and from the power of Satan unto God .... Here I found not a few who seemed to have passed from death to life under your ministry, and who, in addition, had got beyond that ice-cold region of formal profession, in which even those who are alive unto God are afraid to speak above their breath of any of the gracious exercises of the regenerate soul, which so much offend because they so holily condemn a secure but godless generation of carnal professors.'

Soil and atmosphere were ready; and it is no marvel, it is in harmony with God's great and precious promises and with the axiomatic principles of His kingdom, that the fruits in which He rejoices should reveal themselves. Almost as soon as William Burns entered on his task they were disclosed. The church had been full before, but the crowds were denser and more eager than ever. They hung upon him listening, as in Galilee they hung upon those lips which spake as never man spake. The simplicity of the message, its unsparingness and its edge, the conviction which held every one that the preacher was uttering only what his Lord had given him to say – these produced instantaneous effects. Men were over-awed. They knew that God had drawn near them. They expected 'some sudden matter'.

One after another went to Burns to acquaint him with the spiritual benefit they were receiving. He was afraid to hearken; he dreaded that such confidences might prove fuel to feed his complacency and pride. 'On the 6th of June, A.M. came with joy to tell me that she had found her own case all opened up the last two Sabbaths, and that she now found herself as under Mr. McCheyne's ministry. I told her not to cast sparks from hell into my inflammable heart, to give thanks to God, and to beware of commending man.' He dealt more rigorously with himself than with any one else; he was fierce and determined in his antagonism to his own moods; he trembled daily lest he should be tempted to abandon the Valley of Humiliation, where the Lord once had His country-house, and where His servants are most sure of meeting Him still.

Yet the first four months of his residence in Dundee were merely a preface to the better things which later months were to bring. Towards the end of July he left St. Peter's to assist his father in Kilsyth at the dispensation of the Lord's Supper, and, before his return on the 8th of August, he had passed through one of the supreme experiences of his life.

The usual Sacramental services were finished. He had preached on the Sabbath evening, 'without remarkable assistance or remarkable effects'. But, as he closed, there came over him an uncontrollable anxiety for the salvation of these neighbours and friends among whom he had spent his own early years. He intimated that he would address them again in the market-place on Tuesday forenoon at ten o'clock, intending to set out later in the same day on his journey back to Dundee.

Tuesday morning dawned, 'a morning fixed from all eternity in Jehovah's counsels as an era in the history of redemption'. During the previous night godly people in Kilsyth had forgotten to sleep, so busy they were in prayer; for many weeks William Burns himself had taken no rest and given his Lord no rest, because the requirements of St. Peter's taught him his need of more of the supernal strength and wisdom and compassionateness of the Holy Spirit.

The day threatened rain, and it was thought better to gather the crowd that had assembled in the market into the capacious church. Seats, stairs, passages, and porches were thronged by men, women and children, all in their ordinary clothes, and among them some of the wickedest and most profligate of the whole countryside. They sang the 102nd Psalm; and when the speaker read the lines,

> Her time for favour which was set,
> Behold, is now come to an end,

the word *Now* touched his own heart, and encouraged the hope that God's set time was actually at hand.

The text was chosen from another Psalm, the 110th – *Thy people shall be willing in the day of Thy power*. It was a sermon orderly in arrangement, expository, Calvinistic in its teaching, to which the auditors listened with riveted attention and with silent tears. As it drew to its conclusion, Burns described some of those visitations of the Spirit that, again and again, have made a sunshine in the shady places of the Church's pilgrimage; and, among them, the revival at the Kirk of Shotts in 1630, when young John Livingston preached, and when five hundred souls left their charnel-cave for the marvellous liberty of Christ's freemen.

Going on with the relation, he felt himself captured, uplifted, and multiplied by the powers of the Holy Ghost. He was led, like Livingston, to entreat the unconverted before him instantly to close with God's offer of mercy; and he continued doing this, till the emotions of the people became too strong for restraint, and they broke forth in weeping and wailing, cries and groans.

It was three o'clock in the afternoon before the meeting could be dismissed, and the church was empty; and for Burns himself there could be no thought of returning to Dundee that evening, nor for some time afterwards; here was God's work allotted him which he must not desert.

That was the inauguration in Kilsyth of many days of heaven upon the earth. Soon the forsaken public-houses, the dark underworld of the coal-pits, the fields where the reapers and gleaners praised God among the stooks, the weavers' work-shops, the quiet haughs and glens, were all signs and testimonies that the age of Christ's miracles is not past, but that still, as of old, He cleanses the leper, and gives the blind their sight, and raises the dead, and preaches the Good News to the poor.

From this wonderland of grace Burns betook himself again to St. Peter's, the same man and not the same, cast down to a yet lowlier self-abnegation and lifted up to a yet more invincible certitude that with God nothing is impossible. But now, as David Brainerd wrote in his Journal of the *Mirabilia Dei inter Indicos*, so he had his Journal, which recorded 'the Lord's Marvellous Doings for me and many other Sinners at Dundee, 1839'.

The very week which saw him once more at his post was marked by the forth-putting of the right hand of the Most High. At the Thursday evening meeting he explained why he had been absent longer than he had designed, and invited those to remain who were seeking for themselves the way of peace. About a hundred stayed; and 'at the conclusion of a solemn address to their anxious souls, suddenly the power of God seemed to descend, and all were bathed in tears'.

Friday night brought a still more memorable unveiling of the divine majesty and mercy. There was an evangelistic service in the church, and, after it, an adjournment to the vestry. But it was too small for the numbers who pressed in – tempestuous souls taking the Kingdom of Heaven by force. Not one among them but was in deep distress; and with some the anguish of spirit was so masterful, that they could neither stand nor sit nor kneel, but threw themselves prostrate on the floor.

Evening after evening these scenes were repeated, for, through many weeks, the meetings were held every night. In a short time they became so large that they had to assemble in the open air, first in the Meadows, and then, when the magistrates forbade, in the churchyard of St. Peter's, where the field of the dead was transformed into a birthplace of sinning and repenting and sorrowing and rejoicing men.

Burns had numerous helpers in those exacting and heart-melting days – Mr. Roxburgh and Mr. Baxter and Mr. Macalister, Alexander Somerville and James Hamilton and Robert Macdonald and Horatius Bonar and Patrick Miller.

But, as the Journal demonstrates, he stood himself in the glowing centre of the flame. 'I ran up to renew the charge on Satan's hosts,' it says; and again, 'I was led to speak in very plain terms of many prevailing sins'; and, 'There were many crying bitterly, one fell down, and, when I was near the end, I stopped and sat down in silent prayer for five minutes, that all might be brought to the point of embracing Jesus'.

Twenty, thirty, forty would come to him in a single day, asking the old question of the Philippian jailer, *What must we do to be saved*? They 'gathered in little groups in an outer chamber and poured out their hearts in united prayer, or in silent and solitary breathings, as they waited each their turn for a solitary interview'. Sometimes these Seekers – who are the next best sect to the Finders, as the Lieutenant-General of the Parliament wrote to his beloved daughter, Bridget Ireton – kept him occupied till far on in the night. Sometimes they followed him from a meeting, and he had to stop and pray with them 'on the highwayside, under the starlight faintly shining through the dark, windy clouds'.

Was he spoiled by such excitements, opportunities, and privileges? No, for he ascribed all the praise to Christ, and he had an ever-increasing conviction of his own unworthiness. At '20 minutes to 12' on a Saturday evening in September, after 'what a week of mercy and grace and love!' this was his self-accusing prayer, 'O scatter the clouds and mists of unbelief which exhale afresh from the stagnant marshes in my natural heart, the habitation of dragons'; and this was his adoring song, 'Glory to Thee, O Lamb of God! and to Thee, O Father! and to Thee, O Holy Ghost, eternal and undivided!' William Burns knew and was persuaded that he had nothing which he had not received.

It was the rumour of these 'dews from on high' which reached McCheyne in Hamburg, and which filled with thankfulness the last hours of his wanderings. Back in Dundee, he soon had ample evidence of the reality of the awakening.

Six or seven reports remain to us, which were furnished to him at his own request, in the December of this year of grace, by members of the congregation. They give an account of the various private prayer-meetings which had been begun under the impulse of the revival. The penmanship of most of them is poor; the spelling of one or two is lamentably faulty; but they bring a mist over the reader's eyes, and they beget the longing in his soul for just such apocalypses and theophanies and triumphs as they commemorate.

Mrs. Likely speaks of a little meeting for women which gathers in her sick-room; and rejoices over 'many brought to Christ of whom Mr. Burns never knew, and a great number more under your own ministry', whom none had dreamt of until this present time; and covets for her 'dearly beloved pastor a clear discerning judgment' that he may discriminate 'the counterfeit from the coin'.

Agnes Crow remembers how often Mr. McCheyne had wished that his church might 'become a Bochim, a place of weepers'; and, since 'the Spirit of God came among us and broke the rocky hearts in pieces', tears have stolen down 'the cheeks that never were seen to weep for sin before'.

Andrew Cant presides on Sabbath mornings at seven o'clock, and on those Sabbath evenings when there is no service in the church, over 'a meeting held for praise, prayer, and mutual edification in the house of Louisa Lindsay, Tait's Lane, Hawkhill'; and he puts on record the names of those who attend.

David Kay is interested in no less than three similar meetings.

There are two children's prayer-meetings, for the direction of one of which Thomas Sime is responsible, while Thomas Brown cares for the other; and the boys and girls set down their names, and hope that their minister will visit them soon.

Was it surprising that, *when he came and had seen the grace of God, he was glad*?

CHAPTER 7

A Plentiful Rain and the Plenteous Harvest

Dr. Bonar tells us that McCheyne was 'naturally ambitious'; and perhaps – who knows? – some inward regrets assailed him, and some conflicts had to be fought on the hidden Esdraelon of his heart, before he was able to express and to feel nothing but pure and unmingled joy in the fact that God was saving his people by another agent than himself. But the regrets, if ever they presented themselves, were dismissed immediately; and the conflicts, thanks to the mightiness within him of the Leader and Perfecter of his faith, ended almost before they began.

Back once more in the old place of duty, he wrote to his father and mother, on the 26th of November, 1839, a letter instinct with charity, with self-sacrifice, and with gratitude. 'The first sight of Dundee was animating and refreshing to me, and I felt wonder and thankfulness at the way by which God had led me since I bade it farewell. Mr. Nielson, Mr. Thoms, Alexander Thain, and Robert Macdonald of Blairgowrie were waiting to receive me; many also of my dear people. I preached the same evening. I never saw such an assembly in a church before. Mr. Roxburgh, Mr. Arnot, Mr. Low, Mr. Hamilton, and other ministers, came to support me. There was not a spot in the church left unoccupied; every passage and stair was filled. I was almost overpowered by the sight, but felt great liberty in preaching from 1 Corinthians 2:1-4. I never preached to such an audience, so many weeping, so many waiting for the words of Eternal Life. I never heard such sweet singing anywhere, so tender and affecting, as if the people felt they were praising a present God.

'When I came out, the whole of the Church Road was filled with old and young, and I had to shake hands twenty at a time. A multitude followed me to my door, so that I had to speak to them again and pray before sending them away. There is evidently a great change upon the people here; and, though it is to be expected that many are merely naturally awakened and excited, yet I see a great many who, I feel confident, are savingly changed.

'On Sabbath I made Burns preach in the morning and evening, and I preached in the afternoon. It was a very solemn day. 2 Chronicles 5:13, 14, was my text; and Burns preached on *The Throne of Grace*, Hebrews 4. He is certainly a very remarkable preacher. The plainness and force of his statements, and his urgency, I never saw equalled. He has a very clear view of divine things, and an amazing power of voice and body. But, above all, God seems really to accompany his preaching with demonstration of the Spirit. I found him in private much more humble and single-hearted than I could have believed from the reports circulated. We have not yet fixed anything as to what he is to do; I pray that we may be guided from on high.

'I have no desire but the salvation of my people by whatever instrument. I have found out many saved under my own ministry that I did not know of before. They are not afraid to come out now; it has become so common a thing to be concerned about the soul.'

In those grey and wind-driven days of November, McCheyne knew the gladness of glorious summer, and gave thanks for the victories God had been winning through William Burns, and had no desire but the salvation of his people by whatever instrument.

No doubt, in St. Peter's, for a little while, *some said, I am of Paul, and some, I of Apollos*; human nature, even when it is in the process of transfiguration by Christ, does not readily bid goodbye to its predilections and preferences. James Hamilton writes of those who 'almost deprecated an event which would supersede the man who had been to them as an angel of God, and who scarcely concealed their disappointment at their own pastor's arrival'. But, he adds, 'through the sweetness and magnanimity afforded to himself and Mr. Burns the trial passed away'. When Paul and Apollos are themselves determined that there shall be no quarrel, when they are baptized into His own lowliness by the meek and generous Spirit who loves the background and will not speak of Himself and glorifies Jesus only, then, perforce, envies and jealousies, rivalries and contentions, become ashamed and must hide their forbidding heads.

Burns behaved as chivalrously and self-forgettingly as McCheyne. It is difficult to conceive of finer reading than that which is provided by the twenty-seven or twenty-eight letters penned by him to the minister of St. Peter's during the next three years. They are a sort of revelation of his soul, fiery in the fervour of its satisfaction with a 'full and running-over' Christ, panting and thirsting for the conversion of men, trampling its own pridefulness down and willing that it should be crushed to dust and powder, crying at times out of the depths of conscious poverty and impotence. 'I am indeed a cumberer of the ground,' he confesses; and again and again, with those self-accusations which inflict a sorer wound than any flagellant's whip, he scourges his 'stupid heart'.

But McCheyne is always his 'dear brother in Jesus'. He 'loves him in the Lord'. 'Your precious note,' he declares, 'was a cordial sent by the Lord to my fainting soul.' Too long, he protests when his own silence has been more protracted than usual, 'I have been a stranger to one than whom none is nearer my heart'. Or, with one of those rapturous autographs of his, he signs himself, 'Yours in eternal bonds (Glory be to the Lamb!)'. He would not have his friend speak only smooth things, and encouraging messages, to him; his longing to have his dangers and his faults made clearer to himself, by one in whose spiritual insight and skill he could trust implicitly, is very touching and very noble. 'Do not think that I tire of rebukes,' he wrote from Perth in January, 1840; 'if you want my love in Christ, O be faithful to me, that I may not fall into the snare of the devil.' From Aberfeldy, in the end of August, he proffered again the same request: 'O remember me at the Throne of Mercy, and send me faithful counsel'.

If McCheyne was naturally ambitious, Burns, with that flaming energy which had taken farewell of leisure, and which hastened from campaign to campaign, was probably tempted to imperiousness and assertion. But he craved any regimen which would melt him into the humility and patience of Him who *emptied Himself and took the form of a bondservant*; and McCheyne, rich where he was poor and qualified by that unlikeliness to supply his want, must help him to learn better the secret of Jesus Christ.

How the fire kindled at Kilsyth and Dundee spread throughout Scotland, these letters of William Burns to Robert McCheyne recount in their author's nervous and impetuous English. He who reads them recalls Lord Macaulay's picture of the beacon-lights which dispelled the darkness on the night of the Armada's arrival. They shone, those lights, 'from Eddystone to Berwick bounds, from Lynn to Milford Bay', high on St. Michael's Mount, and high on Beachy Head. 'Along each southern shire the Spaniard saw, cape beyond cape, the twinkling points.' Then, from the hills of Surrey and from Hampstead's swarthy moor, they flew and bounded towards the north, until, at last, 'the red glare on Skiddaw roused the burghers of Carlisle'; and a nation was awake to shatter 'the great fleet invincible'. Like that, through 1840 and a segment of 1841, the gleam and glow of the Evangel, as Burns preached it, sped over Scotland. And everywhere men were startled from their sleep, and began to live.

First, it was Perth that was mysteriously and irresistibly stirred. He had gone to St. Leonard's Church there, to help John Milne, recently ordained over the parish. An absence from Dundee of a few days' duration was all that he had planned for himself; in reality, 'the appearance of the Presence of the Lord Emmanuel in His ordinances here' detained him in Perth for more than three months. 'Last night,' he told McCheyne on the 30th of December, 1839, 'the work was so glorious that hardly one out of about a hundred and fifty seemed free from deep impressions of the Word and Spirit of Jesus, and many were evidently pricked in their hearts, while some heavy-laden souls emerged into the liberty of the children of God.' On the 24th of January in the new year, he had more to report: 'I had about thirty young men with me last night seeking conversation and prayer, whose cases, so far as I went into examination, were very interesting and entirely the fruit of the present work'. Rapidly, pregnantly, the details were set down; this was a messenger for whom the King's business always required haste; 'I have not a moment to spare' – it is the formula with which he concludes two of the letters from Perth.

In the opening week of June he wrote from a new district, 'poor, parched Fife, the Valley of the Shadow of Death'. But, a month afterwards, he had 'a good day in Anstruther', and the murkiness of the dispiriting Valley was lifted somewhat. 'It was to many of us very affecting and delightful to see the whole population, with many from surrounding places, assembled together, during the afternoon and evening, at the tent in the churchyard; the dissenting bodies having of their own accord shut up their own places of worship. The Lord's people did indeed seem to be *all one* in Christ. Praise to the Name!'

August and September found him among the hills and moors of Breadalbane; and now the victories of the Golden Prince were well-defined and conspicuous. 'The six weeks just concluded,' his Captain Credence declares, 'have been among the most remarkable that I have ever enjoyed in a public capacity. I have been at Lawers and Ardeonaig on Loch Tay-side, at Fortingall, Aberfeldy, Grandtully, Logierait, Moulin, Tenandry, and Kirkmichael; and in hardly any of these places have we been left without tokens of the Lord's gracious presence. It seemed, as Mr. Campbell of Lawers said, to be like a resurrection, the work of the Spirit was so extended, powerful, and independent of the means employed. I never saw God moving more evidently in a sovereign manner. In many cases I have found it eminently necessary, and much blessed, to ask those anxious to wait at the close of a public meeting, in order to get nearer their consciences, and bring them to a stand as to the offer of a free salvation. But, here, this was not needed. The Lord carried on His work mightily during the ordinary services; and I always found it most desirable to leave the people instantly, after the blessing was pronounced, and send them to a secret meeting with the Lord.'

It was wonderful, too, how God had inclined the Moderate ministers, in these parts of Perthshire, to welcome to their parishes and pulpits such a Son of Thunder and of Consolation. Nothing could have been more gracious than the courtesy of Mr. Macdonald of Fortingall, Mr. Campbell of Moulin, and Mr. Buchanan of Logierait; the last of the trio was 'very friendly and very serious', even though 'we were at the Tent without interruption during five hours, and the power of the Word in the hand of the Spirit was so great that hundreds were in tears and many cried aloud'. Burns entreated McCheyne to join himself 'in wrestling with the Lord that He may pour out His fullness' on these kindly outsiders, who might so soon have the Veil lifted to them and the way opened into the Holiest of all.

But, once again, he remembered his own constant necessity. 'You have drawn me to a sweet duty, but one that compels me to be egotistical. May the Lord save me from the accompanying danger to my poor soul, and do you pardon me, and pray for me more and more that I may lie as clay in the hands of the Potter, at the feet of Emmanuel.'

In Aberdeen, from which the next dispatches are sent, the fight is more uphill. 'I can say but little that is good' – this was written on the 17th of October – 'though still there is room for prayerful hope. The mass of church-going professors seem to be almost stereotyped. And, after continuing during those ten days past to preach, as Dr. Chalmers would say, on the principle of "attraction" to such as chose to come, I last night adopted the plan of assembling the poor and abandoned in a school-house. We seemed to have more of the Lord's presence there than at the meetings in church; and, when I was leaving, the passage, *I will move them to jealousy with them which are not a people*, struck me very forcibly, and also the Parable of the Marriage Feast.'

Nearly a year later – for it is impossible to enumerate all the beacon-fires, and the narrative must hurry on – Burns had turned southward, and was across the Border in Newcastle, a heavenlier raid than the Douglases and Armstrongs of the older time. 'O stir up the people to plead for us here!' he begged. 'There is progress making, though as yet slow. We are coming to the crisis; and I have hope that something great may yet be done by Him who only doth wondrous things.'

To his friend, that through him it might be conveyed to 'the children of God in Dundee', he entrusted a call to united prayer, which, in its Rembrandtesque gloom, its sententious vigour, and its white heat, reminds us of some of Cromwell's letters when Puritan and Cavalier were waging their long drawn-out and deadly battle. 'I send these lines to put you in remembrance of all that we have seen and tasted together at the hand of our God and Father, and to entreat you, for the glory of God, to remember without ceasing in your prayers the cause of the Lord Jesus here. This town is like Sodom, abandoned to utter ungodliness and enormous wickedness. Satan's trenches are deep and wide; his walls are strong and high; his garrison is great and fearless; and all that man can do is but like arrows shot against a tower of brass. O, what is to be done? Beloved, I do not need to tell *you*. *You* have *known* that God the Spirit is omnipotent, and can, with a touch of His finger, make His enemies quail, and raze their fortresses to the ground. O, how glorifying to Him that the walls of Jericho should fall at the blast of a ram's horn! That the mountains should be thrashed to dust and fanned into the air by a worm! Come, believers, let us look to the Lord. Let us stand still, in an agony of desire and hope, that we may see God's salvation .... The battle is beginning. The enemy will not give way without a dread struggle. Hold up our hands; give the Lord no rest; and look for news of victory in due time.'

To listen to William Burns is to be ashamed of our otiose prayers, our sinewless faith, our contracted sacrifices, and our easy and bloodless zeal.

It would indeed brace us stupendously to commit those fusile letters to memory, and to carry them in our souls. On New Year's Day, in 1842, he was in Leith – 'three and a half hours in the open air', and 'the impression was so great that we could have continued much longer'. The following Sabbath, for nearly three hours, he preached at the pier-head to a vast crowd of non-churchgoers; 'it is affecting to see so many young men drawn to hear the Lord in such circumstances; and I hope it is not in vain'.

Two months later, in Edinburgh, he was the head and front of an unrelenting war against the Railway Company, which had started the running of a Sabbath train. It was advertised to leave the station at seven o'clock in the morning; but 'if the Lord enable me, I am to be there in good time, to give tracts to all comers, and to preach at their very gates after the train is off; and this I intend to continue as long as I remain here'. He wished that he could have McCheyne by his side, for, in opposing this violation of God's law, his friend was as ardent as he was himself; but 'let them come on! – one thousand shall flee at the rebuke of one; two shall put ten thousand to flight!'

The penultimate letter of the series – the final one of all must be reserved for a subsequent page – was sent from Largo on December 16, 1842. It is as memorable as any of its pred-

ecessors. The writer has in view the impending Disruption
of the Church, and is much concerned that he and his fel-
low-worker in Dundee should make the most of the breath-
ing-space before the storm breaks. 'What are you thinking
in regard to a general diffusion of the gospel over the land by
evangelistic labour? Is the Lord, do you think, preparing you
for this either in outward circumstances or in inward bias?
Whatever is to be done, must it not be done speedily? – for,
when ministers leave their churches empty in the country
parts, we cannot hope that liberty will long be given to any
of us to interfere with the peace – accursed peace! – of their
successors. In the meantime every day is precious.' So he
goes on to narrate how, though it is midwinter, he could not
keep from itinerating, and had been now for an exact month
in Fife with his hands more than full.

There is a touch of mischief in the next sentences: 'The
pulpit even of Mr. Milligan at Elie has been twice open to
me on weeknights, on the latter of which, as the opportunity
was rare, I did not vacate it for five hours! Happily he was
from home, and could not interfere.' At Largo, where Mr.
Brown was on the right side, though the presence of the Lord
the Spirit was not so incontestably mighty as William Burns
had seen elsewhere, 'the meetings are deeply solemn as well
as crowded, and I hear of not a few who are under some
anxiety about their state'. As for himself, if the parish kirk
was not granted him, he rejoiced that other doors stood wide.
'I preach in all kinds of churches – Independent, Secession,
Relief; and the union of hearts among God's true people is
sweet indeed. The scattered brood must gather under the
mother's wing when the night is coming on, and she summons them with a peculiar note which they understand.'

The long letter draws to its close; but, when it has been

signed and sealed, it is opened again, and a postscript equally long is added. Will McCheyne not come and stand beside him? And will he not do it at once? 'O, that you and a few more of our brethren were sent forth by the Lord to the field in which I am favoured to be! The people are waiting in the market-place, until some one call them in the name of Jesus. Why should St. Peter's, or any other parish, have shower upon shower, when many districts have not a drop? The time is short. Come away to the help of the Lord, the help of the Lord against the mighty!'

We must run – it was always William Burns's word, until in China, in surroundings very different from those of Scotland and Newcastle, God taught him a second lesson, *We must wait*. Then his education was finished; and he was ready for that perfect estate about which he wrote in an *O Altitudo!* to Robert McCheyne, 'They do not measure hours and days in Heaven! Hallelujah!'

But we must get back to Dundee to see how the fire burned there, and how the life developed and deepened where first it was called forth. The minister of St. Peter's, home from one Holy Land, discovered another among the people in whose service he had toiled before he turned his face Eastward, and for whose salvation he had prayed during all his absence. 'Everything here I have found in a state better than I expected,' he told Andrew Bonar a week or two after the comrades in travel had parted; although he added that, for a season, the Spirit's most palpable and most majestic manifestations appeared to be stayed. Yet he avowed his conviction, too, that God would 'soon return in greater power than ever'. Eternity, he said, seemed very near. So, beyond question, it was.

Two years later, in December, 1841, when once again there

was a proposal to remove him from Dundee – this time to
Kettle in Fifeshire – he refused to entertain the notion, and
he gave the absolutely convincing reason: 'I do not think I
can speak a month in this parish without winning some souls'.
Happy minister and happy people, to whom, as to the Laza-
rus with whom Karshish talked, there was always the spiritual life around the natural life, and from whose Sabbaths
and weekdays God was never far removed! In St. Peter's, in
that desirable day of the Holy Ghost, the unseen and everlasting world kept breaking into the time-world, as the capes
and promontories of a continent jut out into the ocean. Men
saw for themselves its towers and spires, and heard the rav-
ishment of its melodies, and tasted its mystic fruits, and
walked and talked with the Son of God and Son of Man who
is its Lord and King.

That the life went on advancing and ripening we have
good evidence in the brief characterization he gives of his
young communicants during the period – brief, yet revealing
and sacred. But, first, let us set down the questions he dic-
tated to them, 'to be answered in secret to God':

1. Is it to please your father and mother, or any one on
   earth, that you come to the Lord's Table?
2. Is it because your friends and companions are coming? and because it is customary?
3. Is it because you have come to a certain time of life?
4. Who, do you think, should come to the Lord's Table?
   and who stay away?
5. Do you think any should come but those who are truly
   converted? and what is that?
6. Would you come if you knew yourself to be unconverted?

7. Should those come who have had some anxiety, but are not brought to Christ?

8. Do you think you have been awakened? brought to Christ? born again?

9. What makes you think so?

10. What is the meaning of taking the bread and wine into the hand? Have you as truly accepted Christ?

11. What is the meaning of feeding upon them? Do you think you are as truly feeding upon Christ, and deriving your strength from Him alone?

12. What is the meaning of giving them to those beside you at the same Table? Do you thus love the brethren?'

It is a searching scrutiny, a piercing light, a spear of Ithuriel to lay bare the very thoughts and intents of the heart. Having in retirement subjected themselves to the scrutiny, and come to the light's penetration and blaze, and felt the spear's touch of celestial temper 'which no falsehood can endure', the catechumens went to see their minister; and, for the years 1840, 1841, and 1842, we are permitted to read his comments on them, and his account of what he found in them.

There were differences, of course. There were disappointments. Some were unready, still feeling their way towards the Wicket Gate and the Man whose name is Goodwill. Some even were 'hard and insensible'; though, when the minister had to employ such sorrowful adjectives, he was ready to add, 'perhaps from ignorance'. But the proofs were numerous and clear that Christ had been working His signs of power and love, and that He had not yet ceased from the super-human work. The ages of the applicants varied: a few were fourteen, a larger number fifteen, even more sixteen and seventeen, while others were considerably older. And what had

McCheyne to record about them? The names need not be written here; it is his verdict on the heart and the life in which we are interested.

In October, 1840, these are among the entries: 'Anxious to come under William Burns. Seems really a child of God, though it is hard to know'; 'Evidently anxious'; 'Seems really in earnest'; 'I trust has really come to Christ'; 'Has come previously unconverted, now evidently under deep concern'; 'Fine, quiet, staid young woman, well-instructed, seems also under the teaching of the Spirit, very silent'; 'A backslider, re-awakened under prayer, many tears and deep feeling of sin'; 'Seems truly to have got salvation under William Burns'; 'Kept long back because he felt unworthy, now he feels pleasure at the Throne of Grace'.

We go on to March, 1841, to read such things as the following: 'Really taught of God, wept unfeignedly'; 'Sweet Irish girl. "Have you found Christ?" "I hope and trust I have"'; 'Twin sister of the above, answers distinctly and well, can say nothing as to time'; 'Still cares for her soul' – this is a young disciple of fourteen – 'and loves Jesus: "The blood of Christ gives me peace, Christ is precious to me"'; 'Awakened under William Burns, and went back to the world; awakened again at last Communion; I trust there is something of God here; very silent'; 'Truly saved, so far as I can see'; 'A fine serious boy, though, I fear, not established'.

A year afterwards, in April, 1842, we have more of the soul-miniatures: 'Anxious when William Burns was here, but it went away; now concerned again, yet does not seem to lay hold'; 'Seems really in earnest, but trembles to say she has found the Lord Jesus'; 'Seems to have been really brought to Christ within this year in St. Peter's'; 'Seems to have been really saved in St. Peter's within the past year; staid, simple, peaceful'; 'Awakened lately under the Parable of the Ten Virgins; seems really in earnest, but thinks it better to keep back this time'; '"I'm a great sinner, but I believe on Christ"; awakened at Quarterly Sacrament nine months ago'; 'Very attentive and anxious, knowledge not full yet or clear, awakened under W. Burns in Dudhope'; 'Lately awakened very deeply, and since Mr. Bonar spoke to her seems to have found rest'; 'Awakened under my ministry in St. Peter's, since he came a twelvemonth ago from Kilspindie; fine clear knowledge and seemingly heart-grasp of the truth'.

Or let us travel forward, across six months more, to the Communion of October, 1842: 'Thinks she came to Christ over these words, *The cup which My Father hath given Me, shall I not drink it?*'; 'Awakened deeply, thinks she has come to Christ, an interesting case'; 'Has been deeply concerned for a year'; 'Awakened two years ago under my ministry, seems honestly in search of Christ'; 'Wants further instruction, seems truly a child of God'.

Are those rapid, unfinished, broken sentences of little value, bare and unimpressive and dry? On the contrary they are possessed of another quality altogether. Each of them is a door opened into a human heart; each is a magic glass through which we gain illuminating glimpses of a man's or a woman's soul. The soul, we see, is thirsting after the living water, or is newly arrived at the place somewhat ascending where stands a Cross, or has lately tasted the manumission and enlargement wherewith Christ makes the captive free. It is weeping, or it is rejoicing; and its grief and its gladness are over the supreme things, sin and salvation, its own bankruptcy and the unsearchable riches of its Friend and Lord. Compared with these, all other biographies are poor; all secular histories, even the most absorbing, are trifling and tame.

In the Dundee of the time the loss and gain which George
Herbert commemorates were well understood; and what loss
is so desperate? or what gain so rare and perfect? –

> For, as Thy absence doth excell
>   All distance known,
> So doth Thy nearness bear the bell,
>   Making two one.

McCheyne himself seemed refined in those years into a
new holiness and zeal. His sermons, written still with com-
parative fullness, and bearing evidence always of thought
and care, had in them more yearning, more eagerness, and
more of a divine haste to magnify Christ and to move the
hearts and wills of men. Very arresting are the short ejacula-
tions which he got into the habit of appending to them, once
the writing was finished. Now this was the winged arrow of
prayer, 'Lord, incline their hearts to run to Thyself'; or it
was, 'Out of weakness make me strong; send showers of the
Spirit'; or again, 'Awake, O North Wind, awake'; or, 'Own
Thine own truth to the conversion of sinners and comfort of
saints'; or, 'O Life of the world, help me'; or, once more,
'Lord Jesus, help!'.

One recalls the story of Robert Bruce, the Covenanter,
the man whose prayers were short, but each of them 'a strong
bolt shot up to heaven': how, one Sabbath afternoon, in his
church at Larbert – the parish which McCheyne knew so
well – the people were surprised that he did not appear to
begin the service, and sent the officer to look for him in the
little room which was his oratory between sermons, and the
officer halted on the threshold of the room because he overheard an interview proceeding within, and then returned to
the congregation to report that there was Someone with the

minister, and that Master Bruce was protesting earnestly and many times over that he could not and would not go alone into the church, but that this Other must accompany him.

So McCheyne, when he had ended his own preparations for the pulpit, felt that he was still unprepared until he had importuned the same mysterious and ineffable Companion to be with him and to fulfil through him His own good pleasure. To those years, too, belongs that impressive Act of Personal Examination and Reformation which Dr. Bonar has given in full in the *Memoir*, and which the minister of the gospel cannot read too often or ponder too humbly and faithfully. For the sharpening of our penitence and the growth of our grace let us extract some of its sentences:

'I am persuaded that I shall obtain the highest amount of present happiness, I shall do most for God's glory and the good of man, and I shall have the fullest reward in eternity, by maintaining a conscience always washed in Christ's blood, by being filled with the Holy Spirit at all times, and by attaining the most entire likeness to Christ in mind, will, and heart that is possible for a redeemed sinner to attain in this world.'

'I ought to examine my dreams; my floating thoughts; my predilections; my often recurring actions; the slanders of my enemies, and the reproofs, and even banterings, of my friends; to find out traces of my prevailing sin.'

'I ought to confess the sins of my confessions – their imperfections, sinful aims, self-righteous tendency – and to look to Christ as having confessed my sins perfectly over His own sacrifice.'

'I ought to see that in Christ's blood-shedding there is an infinite over-payment for all my sins. Although Christ did not suffer more than infinite justice demanded, yet He could not suffer at all without laying down an infinite ransom.'

'I ought to study Christ as an Intercessor. I am on His breastplate. If I could hear Christ praying for me in the next room, I would not fear a million of enemies. Yet the distance makes no difference. He *is* praying for me.'

'I ought to study the Comforter more – His Godhead, His love, His almightiness.'

'I say, "It is needful to my office that I listen to this, or look into this, or speak of this". So far, this is true; yet I am sure Satan has his part in this argument. I should seek divine direction, to settle how far it will be good for my ministry and how far evil for my soul.'

'I ought not to omit any of the parts of prayer – confession, adoration, thanksgiving, petition, and intercession. Perhaps every prayer need not have all these; but surely a day should not pass without some space being devoted to each.'

'I ought to pray before seeing any one. Often, when I sleep long, or meet with others early, and then have family prayer and breakfast and forenoon callers, it is eleven or twelve o'clock before I begin secret prayer. This is a wretched system.'

'It would stir me up to pray with the map before me.'

These are words which no one can read without realizing that this man was at home and in tune with God, or without discovering why the trumpet of the Lord on his lips, now the iron trumpet and then the silver one, compelled the wanderers back from the far country to the Father's house. He speaks, in his Act of Examination, of his intercessions. They became more and more systematic, and more and more intense. We find his scheme for them detailed and unfolded in one of his notebooks. He has four circles which he fills with prayer. The smallest is that of his kinsfolk; outside this, there is that of intimate friends; then that of his congregation; then, largest of all, the great circle of the ministry, which stretches and expands from Dundee and Larbert and Edinburgh and Blairgowrie and Collace and Anderston and Kelso to the very ends of the earth – to the missionaries in India, in China, in Africa, in Roman Catholic lands, and among the Jews.

Let us examine, for it concerns us particularly, the third of the circles, that which encloses and embraces his congregation. There are no fewer than eleven separate classes into which the people are divided. What are the first four?

'The careless' – he will beg and cry for their arousal, and will refuse to let God go till the blessing is bestowed.

'The anxious' – and thirteen names are set down of men and women asking the road to Zion, whom he will aid to reach the City by soliciting and supplicating the King of the way on their behalf.

'Those brought to peace' – and now there are nineteen names, and on his knees he halts and pauses over each, to isolate it from its neighbours and to give thanks.

'The Christians', about whose Christianity there is no manner of doubt, who are his fellow-soldiers in the Holy War – and ten names succeed, and, as he remembers them one by one, his prayers first climb into praises, and then return to requests that these friends of his own heart and of Christ's heart may know more adequately still *what is the exceeding greatness of God's power to usward who believe.*

Ay, it is not a surprise that 'eyes rekindling' followed McCheyne's steps, that he was daily used of his God to 'recall the stragglers' and 'refresh the outworn', and that to him

> ... it was given
> Many to save with himself;
> And, at the end of the day,
> A faithful shepherd, to come,
> Bringing his sheep in his hand.

In December, 1840, the Presbytery of Aberdeen appointed a committee to investigate the movements of revival which were stirring the country. This chapter of our history may close with a quotation from McCheyne's reply to the Presbytery's queries.

'By far the most remarkable season of the working of the Spirit of God in this place,' he says, 'was in 1839, when I was abroad. Those who were privileged to be present at these times will, I believe, never forget them.

'Since my return, however, I have myself frequently seen the preaching of the Word attended with so much power, and eternal things brought so near, that the feelings of the people could not be restrained. I have observed at such times an awful and breathless silence pervading the assembly; each hearer bent forward in the posture of rapt attention; serious men covered their faces to pray that the arrows of the King of Zion might be sent home with power to the hearts of sinners. Again, at such a time, I have heard a half-suppressed sigh rising from many a heart, and have seen many bathed in tears. At other times I have heard loud sobbing in many parts of the church, while a deep solemnity pervaded the whole audience. I have also, in some instances, heard individuals cry aloud, as if they had been pierced through with a dart.

'These solemn scenes were witnessed under the preaching of different ministers, and sometimes occurred under the most tender gospel invitations. On one occasion, for instance, when the minister was speaking tenderly on the words, *He is altogether lovely*, almost every sentence was responded to by cries of the bitterest agony.[1] At such times, I have seen

---

1. There is a story, also, of how, when McCheyne was preaching on 'The Church a Garden and Fountain' – the outline of the sermon is in the *Memoir and Remains* – he began by saying that he meant that day to

persons so overcome that they could not walk or stand alone. I have known cases in which believers have been similarly affected through the fullness of their joy. I have often known such awakenings to issue in what I believe to be real conversion. I could name many of the humblest, meekest believers, who at one time cried out in the church under deep agony. I have also met with cases where the sight of souls thus pierced has been blessed by God to awaken careless sinners who had come to mock.

'I am far from believing that these signs of deep alarm always issue in conversion, or that the Spirit of God does not often work in a more quiet manner. Sometimes He comes like the pouring rain; sometimes like the gentle dew.

'Still I would humbly state my conviction that it is the duty of all who seek the salvation of souls, and especially the duty of ministers, to long and pray for such solemn times, when our slumbering congregations shall be made to cry out, *Men and brethren, what shall we do?*'

Yes, yes! Come from the four winds, O Breath of God!

---

speak to believers, but that there was no reason why those outside should not have a glimpse, across the walls and through the bars of the gate, of the delights of the place. And this hint, of their impoverishment and exile, stirred more than one to seek and find admission to the 'Garden enclosed' and the 'Fountain sealed'.

CHAPTER 8

To the End o' the Day and the Last Load Home

1

The field of McCheyne's usefulness widened as the years went forward. After his return from the Holy Land, he counted no time lost which was spent in advocating the cause of Christian missions among the Jews, and he was ready to go anywhere to address men and women on the subject of their duty to Israel. And then, when the dews and rains of revival fell in connection with his congregation, many were eager to hear from his lips the story of God's gracious remembrance of His people, hoping that in their corner, too, of His great vineyard there might be granted the April of blossom and the autumn of fruit.

More than once he travelled to Ireland to publish his double message, which perhaps is not double so much as single, because in a home-church that has been quickened from above a new enthusiasm is inevitably born for the ingathering of Jew and Gentile to the fold of the one Shepherd of the sheep.

He was still busy, moreover, with his endeavours on behalf of Church Extension; so that these two words, as William Burns informs us, were given as name and title to his pony: and was it the Tullia of the old days, or some successor, that trotted on her master's errands with the same untiring fidelity and plodding perseverance?

But another clarion-summons sounded now in his ears,

and moved him to the depths of his being. Those were the eventful years when the Disruption of the Scottish Kirk was impending. In the Assembly the majority was at length evangelical, determined that Christ alone should bear rule in His own realm and society of believing souls. Throughout the country quiet and God-fearing men held a similar conviction. They were Non-Intrusionists, and the doctrine of Spiritual Independence was dearer to them than life itself. But, alike in the Assembly and in the country, numbers remained of the opposite opinion; and the debate between the parties had come to the critical stage. For, in case after case, ministers had been forced by patrons on congregations, against the wishes of most of the members, and in defiance of the decisions of the Presbyteries; and the Erastian interference with the liberties of Christ's freemen had still its defenders within the Church and throughout the land.

What made matters more serious was that the Judges of the Civil Courts, when the disputed settlements were referred to their arbitrament, were decreeing, not indeed unanimously but by majorities, that congregations and presbyteries must bow to the will of the patrons, and must accept the ministers whom they themselves disliked and distrusted. And where, if these decrees were carried out, were the high and inalienable privileges of the citizens in Christ's kingdom? Where the headship of Christ Himself over the commonwealth which He had bought with His blood?

Thus, in the Scotland of the time, the opposing ranks confronted each other, and the battle was joined, and soon the Church was to be rent in two, brave and godly people preferring to go out from the old ecclesiastical home rather than bate a jot of their Heavenly Master's rights or suffer any infringement of His dignity and rule.

There never was a doubt in McCheyne's mind as to the side on which the truth lay. He was a convinced and ardent Non-Intrusionist. He did not see the actual Disruption with its sacrifices and its splendours, except it were from the lofty walls of the New Jerusalem; but, if he had lived, he would have ranged himself in the great company which marched from St. Andrew's Church to Tanfield Hall on the 18th of May, 1843. When, a few days before his death, Mr. Fox Maule brought the question before the House of Commons, he wrote to a friend: 'Eventful night this in the British Parliament! Once more King Jesus stands at an earthly tribunal, and they know Him not'.

But, in November, 1842, he was a member of the historic Convocation, which met in Roxburgh Chapel in the Old Town of Edinburgh. Four hundred and sixty-five ministers, whose sympathies were evangelical, and whose desire was to preserve the independence of the Church, came to it: 'the whole chivalry' of the Kirk, Lord Cockburn said, though there were good men amongst those whose policy was diametrically different.

Robert McCheyne had drawn up the proposal for united prayer, which was disseminated from Caithness to Wigtownshire in prospect of the Convocation; and at its earliest session he was one of those who led the devotions of the gathering. 'We had usually three prayers at every diet,' Dr. Guthrie writes, 'and I never heard such and so many remarkable prayers.'

In a little pocket notebook, in pencil, and in a handwriting even more diminutive and microscopic than usual, McCheyne has delineated, through seven-and-twenty engrossing pages, the speakers and the incidents of the memorable week.

On Thursday, November 17th, we read, 'Dr. Chalmers

preached in St. George's to an immense multitude, and old Mr. Macdonald prayed'. It is a significant grouping of names, a *par nobile fratrum*. One was the greatest Scotsman of his time – a man, Dr. James Hamilton declared, 'who might so easily have been the Adam Smith, the Leibnitz, and the Bossuet of the day, but who, having obtained a better part, laid economics and philosophy and eloquence on the altar which sanctified himself'. The other, Dr. John Macdonald of Ferintosh, was 'the Apostle of the North' – orator, evangelist, and saint – who held the Highlands in the hollow of his hand; who felt that the supreme thing in preaching is the presentation of Christ; who, freed from entangling fears about himself, carried a sustaining joyousness of spirit with him into all his work: 'from St. Kilda to Tarbat Ness, from Kinlochbervie to Ardeonaig,' says Dr. William Macgregor, 'there was not a parish which had not known his power.'[1]

After this opening ceremonial the first evening was preliminary; and, looking through our annalist's eyes, we are spectators of the scene in Roxburgh Chapel. Chalmers presides, and Thomas Pitcairn of Cockpen has been appointed clerk; and Dr. Duncan of Ruthwell, the founder of Savings Banks, and then McCheyne himself, have poured forth the confessions and thanksgivings and supplications of the assembly. Afterwards the chairman counsels his listeners to give free utterance to their sentiments, for their one object in coming together is frank deliberation, and the mind of the Church must be thoroughly ascertained; therefore let there be a colloquial style in speech, and as near an approximation as possible to table-talk.

Immediately the table-talk begins; and what giants they are who participate in it! Dr. Macfarlan of Greenock, who,

---

1. *Our Church in the Highlands*, p. 7.

when the wrench comes, will leave for conscience' sake the wealthiest benefice in the Church; Dr. Paterson, who wrote of the Manse Garden; old Dr. Burns of Kilsyth, the father of our evangelist with the burning and bleeding heart; and Alexander Keith, and James Buchanan, and Henry Moncrieff, and Robert Candlish. The last is specially good to hear. He insists on the need of prayer to Almighty God. 'We may be of one mind, and yet there will be much diversity of opinion. We are men who, of ourselves, cannot see one foot in advance, who stagger blindly, and who must feel our way. What has passed among us tonight proves it. It makes us more than ever diffident of our own wisdom. It should throw us more completely and confidingly on the guidance of God's good Spirit.' And thus, when they have decided on future hours of meeting and adjournment – from eleven to four, and from seven to ten – the initial day draws to its conclusion.

Next morning they are back, and the 72nd Psalm is sung 'with much fervour', and the 60th chapter of Isaiah is read. Then Dr. Macfarlan explains for what purpose they have met. He discusses the greatness of the issues at stake. 'It is not a question of our benefices; that is a drop in the bucket; it is whether the Church of Scotland is to remain the same in its fundamental principles, and whether the supremacy of Christ as its King is to be practically maintained.' We catch the trumpet-note, the strain of the confessors and martyrs, in his last sentence; 'I could not be free to remain a minister of a Church whose chief glory was taken away'.

Once more there is the unfettered table-talk, in which Mr. Begg of Liberton and Mr. Guthrie of Edinburgh take a prominent share; and it grows apparent that one result of the Convocation will be a set of resolutions which unfold to Government and the Houses of Parliament, as well as to the people of the land, what measure and degree of liberty the Church demands as consistent with its truth and honour.

That Friday night, when they have sung the 91st Psalm and read the 14th chapter of Exodus, comforting and kindly Scriptures both, Mr. Begg makes a motion which will have the effect of modifying somewhat these resolutions; and here and there are some who coincide with his view. But Dr. Candlish replies that he 'dare not stand on the abolition of Patronage' as being all that is required – 'we must be set right in our jurisdiction'. So, on Saturday, McCheyne has this to record, that, 'after an amazing speech from Dr. Chalmers, which brought tears into many eyes, 427 agreed to the resolutions'.

Having travelled this far, the ministers, in the beginning of the new week, can consider what they ought to do if the Legislature should refuse them that relief from Intrusion which they have defined and asked. There is substantial agreement. They must forsake the Establishment without more delay. Mr. Begg, indeed, is not certain about the wisdom of crossing the Rubicon so quickly and irremediably: 'If it is duty, then no matter what consequences ensue; but suppose you cannot prove it to be duty? I must exhaust all the means for bringing about the opposite result.' But Charles Brown answers, 'If the State declares its mind that we hold our temporalities on certain conditions which are unlawful', there is nothing for it but that the temporalities must be laid down and left behind. And Thomas Guthrie protests that, 'as an honest man, he cannot take the pay of the State without doing all its bidding', and is persuaded that 'a dinner of herbs where love is' has incalculably more satisfaction in it than the comfort and plenty which are bought by the smallest sacrifice of principle.

To one of the closing sessions, too, Dr. Chalmers, with statesman's prescience and mastery of detail, expounds his scheme of a Sustentation Fund, by which in a free Church the ministry may be adequately supported. He 'will,' he says, 'demonstrate the grounds on which, should the worst come to the worst, the Christianity of these lands may be maintained'; and he fulfils his promise. It can be done, he is convinced, 'not on the strength of great sums, but of little ones'; for '£100,000 will be produced by a penny a week from each family'.[2]

Morning and night, till Wednesday, the 23rd, when the sacred and yet heartsome gathering is consummated, McCheyne follows and recounts its procedure with loving particularity. He knew that it was good to be there. He said his cordial Amen to the dictum of a leader in the table-talk, that 'it were worth while sealing with one's blood' the verdicts of the Convocation.

2

Is the reader wearied of this long trespass through ecclesiastical woods and pastures? But it will be of value if it helps us to an understanding of one phase in McCheyne's character. His name was Mr. Valiant-for-Truth, and there was a militant quality in his religion. He could not brook that harm should be done to Christ's prerogative. He would not suffer any questioning of the authority of conscience, once it has been enlightened by the Word and the Spirit, or any dulling of its susceptivity, or any temporizing with its queenly

2. 'It is astonishing,' said Dr. Chalmers in the Free Church Assembly of 1844, 'the power of infinitesimals: the mass of the planet Jupiter is made up of infinitesimals; and surely, after that, it is in the power of infinitesimals to make up a stipend for the minister of Ballachulish!'

imperative. He, too, was of the stuff of which Hugh Mackail and James Renwick were made. But now we may go back, through a few months from that vital November week, to something which is very beautiful and holy.

In August, 1842, he paid a visit to Ruthwell in Dumfries-shire, the old haunt of his boyhood; and from this visit three of his cousins dated their entrance into the life that is life indeed. With his hand pointing the way and beckoning them on, they seem to have crossed almost simultaneously the boundary-line from the world of nature to the world of grace. Perhaps nothing in all his experience gladdened him so much. 'You do not know,' he wrote afterwards to his father, 'what deep anxieties I have for you all, that it may be well with you in Eternity. The three young ladies at the Cottage are the first of my kindred to whom I have been savingly useful. Their change, is, indeed, very wonderful; and, if they endure to the end, is enough to convince an infidel of the reality of the Holy Spirit's work.'

The story may only be outlined; it is too intimate and too surpassing to be narrated in full. Maria, Charlotte, and Georgiana Dickson stood apparently in some awe of their cousin when he crossed their threshold; they scarcely knew what to expect from one who was distinguished, above all else, for the absoluteness of his devotion to the things which are unseen. But his Christianity, while it was manifestly thorough, was soon discovered to be astonishingly human, brotherly, and attractive. It drew them. It spoke of desirable secrets which they had never learned, and of pleasures which the comforts and happinesses of their life had not been able to impart. No doubt, also, Robert McCheyne talked now and then about the Master to whose enchantments he was himself in thrall, and who had bound on him the vows which it is

a shame a man should not be bound by; his heart was too
Christ-enslaved for his lips ever to keep silence.

The result was what we have seen. Early in September,
after he had gone, Maria sent him a letter – the forerunner of
many letters penned by the three sisters during the seven
months, which were all that were left them to hold inter-
course with the kinsman so near them in blood, and so much
nearer now in the unity of the faith, and the knowledge of
the Son of God. 'You say, it seems like a dream, the precious
week you spent here. I feel, indeed, awakened from a long
dark dream, and I earnestly pray I may be still more awakened and enlightened.' The morning was sweet, but would
not the noonday be better yet?

Later, there was a proposal that the Ruthwell cousins
should visit Eliza and Robert, and with what eagerness it
was welcomed! 'We would willingly walk it,' one of them
avowed. The plan was duly carried out; and Maria tarried
behind in Dundee, when her younger sisters had turned their
faces southward again. That was because her more brooding
and meditative nature could not accept so readily and with
such simplicity as they did the consolations of the Evangel,
and she wished to linger under the tuition which McCheyne
could give her in public as well as in private.

But this angered another sister, who had continued meantime outside all these strange new ebullitions and energies
of life that were revolutionizing the home. 'I do not agree in
thinking it necessary or pleasing in the eyes of God,' she
protested, 'that this world should be converted into "a living
tomb". I hope you will not encourage Maria in remaining
too much by herself. I think the mind dwelling so entirely on
one subject – and that subject one, the more we contemplate
it, the more entangled in its mysteries and obscurities we

become – is liable to affect the brain. I have known many instances of its giving way from the same cause, "religious enthusiasm", or, as the Calvinists say, "wrestling with the Spirit".' The critical and antagonistic voice has a fascination for us; the emphasis of its dissent and the sharpness of its ridicule seem to convey a hint that the heart behind the voice was not quite at its ease. 'Charlotte is still "very zealous", but is rational. I believe it has been a great struggle to her to try to cool down her affection for me, as she had been taught she should only feel a sort of "compassionate" love for the unconverted and keep her true affection for her "Christian friends".' Or let us take the account given of the youngest sister: 'I often think, if you were a Roman Catholic, and had enforced stripes and penance, poor Georgy would have whipped and mortified herself to death'.

The aggressiveness of first love, and its contempt for the distinctions of social rank, were particularly distasteful to the objector's soul. 'I cannot make my sisters understand that they are far too young to be encouraged prowling about the Parish, talking to all the ploughmen and women on religion and conversion. The sort of feeling of equality there is too much of in Scotland is hateful to me. The lower orders are very well in their way, but should be kept in their proper place. You will say, "What pride! We are all alike in the eyes of God." So we are; but, as long as we are in this world, it is our duty to keep up the distinctions of rank. If not, I should fear having some brothers-in-law in the shape of pious tallow-chandlers, or tinkers, or ploughmen, presented to me, and then told they were Christians and therefore far better than my unconverted self.'

Yes, it is impossible not to be interested in this candid, clever, acidulous, uncompromising, aristocratic adversary.

She tells Robert McCheyne that he must not think her 'like "the woman at the well" – throwing up embankments'; yet it does appear as if conscience and the Holy Ghost were robbing her of rest, in order to lead her, no less than her sisters, by a way that she knew not, to the Rest-giver.

Palpably, however, the freshly-enrolled disciples had some difficult lessons set them from the commencement of their schooling; but, so long as we are permitted to follow its course, their education went steadfastly forward. They encountered a poignant bereavement ere long;[3] and by God's grace they came unharmed and enriched through the trial. There is pathos in the last glimpse we have of the trio. On Monday morning, March 27th, 1843, they were up at an early hour – it is half-past six, one of them notes – to write and dispatch messages in which we catch a sobbing anxiety. They had just heard that their cousin was dangerously ill, and they sent their inquiries and prayers. The truth was that his spirit had passed from the world two days before.

3

He was often absent from his home and parish during the last months of his life. The visit to Ruthwell, from which such golden harvests sprang, had followed one of these absences. With four *true yokefellows* – Purves of Jedburgh, Alexander Somerville of Anderston, Cumming of Dumbarney, and Horatius Bonar of Kelso – he crossed the Border into Northumberland. Newcastle, where William Burns had been before them, was the headquarters of the evangelists. In many instances they preached in the open air.

So it was with the final meeting at which McCheyne him-

---

3. A brother had been killed at Madras by his horse falling upon him.

self was present. To a crowd of a thousand people, gathered in the broad space between the Cloth Market and the cathedral church of St. Nicholas, he spoke of 'the great White Throne'. It was a starry night, and the service went on until ten o'clock, an impressive stillness holding the multitude, and no one moving away. 'We shall never all meet again,' the preacher said as he drew his appeal to its termination, 'till we meet at the Judgment Seat. But these glorious heavens over our heads, and the bright moon that shines on us, and this venerable church behind, are my witnesses that I have set before you life and death.' The watchman had delivered his soul, as in his shortening time he seemed more and more consumingly eager to do.

Much against the will of his elders and people, who were more careful of his health than he was himself, he left Dundee again in the succeeding February, this time by appointment of the Committee of the Convocation. His mission was northward now, to the districts of Deer and Ellon, where Moderatism had reigned in long and almost undisturbed possession, and where there was sore need for the proclamation in its clearness and fullness of the Good News of Christ. A fellow-deputy went with him, the Rev. John Alexander of Kirkcaldy; and, 'for a month all but four days', they were very busy.

In the same tiny notebook in which he has commemorated the meetings of the Convocation, there is a reminiscence of this journey. From a clerical almanac he has cut the printed statistics of the two Presbyteries of Ellon and Deer – the various parishes, the population in each, the ministers with the dates when they were ordained, the patrons; Ellon has eight parish churches, while Deer has thirteen with four chapels-of-ease. These two lists he has gummed on separate

pages into the pocket-book, underlining the places and the
clergymen where a kindly reception might be expected; in
Deer there were five such cases, in Ellon there was but one.
Significant little memoranda are added in pencil: of the days
and hours when the meetings were to be held, of schoolrooms
where the people might gather when the churches were not
available, of homes within which the missioners would find
a welcome if the manse doors were closed. It was toilsome
work, and frequently the weather was of the wintriest.

'I am truly happy to be home after all my wanderings,' he
wrote on the 7th of March from Dundee to his sister, sojourning for the moment in Edinburgh; 'I preached and spoke
twenty-seven times in twenty-four different places, and these
the darkest spots in rugged Scotland.' 'As far as runs the
fallow, as late as holds the light', he scattered with liberal
hand the fine wheat of the kingdom; and, although the soil
looked backward and unpropitious, there were portions of
the field where the seed died, and rooted, and grew, and
brought forth much fruit.

But might it not be his duty to dedicate himself wholly to
this peripatetic and unfettered husbandry? To sunder even
the dear and sacred tie which chained him to St. Peter's?
And to go forth over the country, north and south, east and
west, 'hunting after poor sinners', 'gospelising', 'weeping
out every argument', 'compelling men to cry, Behold how
he loveth us!' – as George Whitefield had done, in England,
in America, and in Scotland too, three-quarters of a century
before? It was an hour in the life of the nation, with the Disruption impending, with old landmarks shaking, when men
and women were specially susceptible to spiritual influences,
when the truth as it is in Jesus required to be explained in its
gracious significance and enforced in its heavenly power,

and when there were not many who could do this as Mc-
Cheyne could. One of his friends at least was convinced that
God meant him now to cut the old bonds at whatever cost,
and to consecrate himself to a wider ministry. From
Kirriemuir, on the 13th of March, William Burns wrote him
a remarkable letter. It must be quoted almost in its entirety.

'Have you got, or are you really seeking, light on your
path? Set apart a day for doing so, with fasting and humiliation. I know not how it is, but it seems more than
clear to me, that you must without delay give up your
charge, and enter on that tempting field in which I am
honoured to be. The fields here are *white*. Calls all around
are coming to me; and I am deceived if there be not the
tokens of an approaching, if not a begun, harvest. Decided good is doing, I hear, in this neighbourhood, at
Lintrathen; and Kirriemuir is ready to move. If you do
not give up your charge, you will please *no* party, and do
nothing in the best way; and your giving up your place on
such a ground, instead of weakening your connection with
the *godly* among your people, will mightily strengthen it.
No doubt, they will make proposals of an *accommodation*, by allowing you to go from home more frequently. I
would not hearken to these. I know from experience that,
until you are *free*, you will not do aright *the work of an
evangelist*, nor make *full* proof of your ministry. In many
cases I might, perhaps, be of use to you as a rough pioneer; and certainly nothing do I see greater need of, in all
places that I go to, than of *you* to enter in and carry on the
work, to which at the best the way is a little smoothed. I
would have you visit the coast of Fife, to which I can
easily make your way plain as far as you need this, and

then come to this quarter. We must *fall upon the shoulders of the Philistines, and spoil them of the East together*. Do not wait for a *Church* call. Christ's call is better. Souls are perishing! Let us to the rescue, and leave others to abide by the *stuff*. You understand me; I do not undervalue *pastoral* work. But there must be a *spiritual* flock *gathered* first. In many places there is *not* this. Remember to be on your guard against the *vis inertiae* of your *fixed* position. Grace and peace. Let me hear soon.'

There – characteristic italics and all – is the well-nigh insupportable and terrible pleading of this 'violent man', who yet was Barnabas as certainly as he was Boanerges. He knew McCheyne's singular and supernatural endowments; he hungered over the derelict souls of men; and he could tolerate no delay. But he kept his letter beside him overnight; and on the next morning, lest it should seem too peremptory, he added a postscript.

'I enclose what I left out in my yesterday's note. May Jehovah graciously and infallibly counsel you in regard to the matter, on which I have ventured, it may be too dogmatically, to advise you. My meaning is, as I said when we met, that, after all, we cannot see with another's eyes. Commit *thy* way to the Lord – this is precious. What would you think of freedom for the six summer months, paying St. Peter's an occasional visit? .... O, we preachers need to *know* God in another way than heretofore, in order to speak aright of sin and of salvation! I am feeling this, and wish I had even the experience of former days. The work of God would flourish by us, if it flourished more richly in us.'

Both in speech and in writing William Burns had urged his view. Was it McCheyne's view also? There is not un-equivocal certainty; but the probabilities are that his opinion coincided with his friend's. When he wrote on March 7th to Eliza in Edinburgh, these were sentences in the letter: 'I think the church should give me a roving commission at once. I can almost say, as Wesley did to the Bishop of London – when he said, "You would be far better with a parish, Mr. Wesley" – "The world is my parish, my Lord." So said a greater than he, *The field is the world.* And soon we shall be cast upon it, if Sir James[4] gets his will.' It is among the might-have-beens, of which there are scores in the regions of history and biography, that, had McCheyne's life been spared through a few weeks longer, he would have resigned his pastorate in St. Peter's, and gone out over broad Scotland to publish and commend the love of God in Christ Jesus our Lord.

4

Robert McCheyne was never married. But, more than once, his sensitive nature was stirred by the heat and tenderness of man's love for woman.

---

4. Sir James Graham, the Home Secretary, whose antagonism to the claims of the Non-Intrusionists was very marked. At first, Dr. Chalmers had good hopes of him. After an interview in 1839, he wrote: 'Sir Robert's extreme caution and coldness operate as a damper on a man's spirits; whereas Sir James is a fine, hearty, honest outspeaking Englishman, of great good feeling and practical sense withal'. But as the Ten Years' Conflict neared its ending, the Home Secretary's opposition to the Evangelicals was undisguised and relentless. He was 'satisfied,' he said in the House of Commons, on March 7th, 1843, 'that any such expectation' as that of the majority in the Church 'never could be realized in any country in which law, or equity, or order, or common sense prevailed'.

When he was a boy of eighteen, he was for a period under its spell. On a former page, some reference was made to Malcolm MacGregor, the close ally of his schooldays. Malcolm had a sister, older than himself, who bore the unusual name of Mondego Mary. They belonged to a Scottish family, that had settled far from the home-country, in the South American town of Bogotà. But the boy was sent to school in Edinburgh, and, for part of the time at least, his sister resided with him, to watch over him and to see to his comfort. Good Mrs. McCheyne, however, was guardian of them both, mothering the strangers with the same assiduous care which she bestowed on the young lives in her own Queen Street nest: there are letters of Malcolm's, written somewhat later, in which he pours out his gratitude in frank and generous words.

Thus the young people saw much of each other; and in the heart of Robert McCheyne a feeling grew up for Mary MacGregor which was warmer than one of friendliness and good comradeship. That she, on her part, was drawn towards him is proved by an album, which first was hers, and then, by her gift, became his. In its pages she has copied out many of his verses in her own beautiful handwriting, the sloping and delicate and fairy-like script of a lady of eighty years ago. Whether, indeed, the affection on her side was as strongly felt as on his may be questioned. She must have been his senior by a number of years, and, one may surmise, did not so readily let herself go; by and by she had a husband in London, and a home of her own.

But for some months he lived, as a young lad will, in his palace of dreams; and she was its queen. For her birthday in 1831 he wrote a set of stanzas, which are tinged with the pensiveness and melancholy that so often assert themselves in his verse, but which make plain the fact of his emotion:

> To weep and smile
> A little while,
> To love, regret,
> Forsake, forget,
> Then be forgotten too –
> This petty strife
> Sums up our life,
> While earth retains
> The soul in chains,
> And heaven is out of view ...
>
> But though our strain
> Be cold and vain,
> And though our joy
> Have much alloy,
> And tears our mirth may vary –
> While hope and fear
> Are mingled here,
> We'll lift on high
> A suppliant eye,
> And bless Mondego Mary.

Much was to happen ere her next birthday arrived. Her sojourn in Edinburgh had come to an end. McCheyne himself had passed through the great spiritual change.[5] He turned again to his harp, 'though long upbound' and discovered that 'the strings yet knew their accustomed sound'. But now, be-

---

5. How complete the spiritual change was is reflected, also, in these lines addressed at this time to Malcolm MacGregor. They are worthy of special remark, because they display a vivacity which is not always present in his verses:

cause Christ controlled him, while she as yet remained unvanquished by this supreme Lover, he could believe that God had reasons for their separation. The new lines are an imitation of Cowper's address to Mary Unwin:

> Mysterious Fate! that one short year
> Should comprehend the whole career
> That we should hold communion here,
>   My Mary!

Thanks, dearest Malcolm, for your kind advice,
Your gentle hints and appellations nice!
But, since 'tis contrary to common sense
To hang a thief not hearing his defence,
I pray you listen to the lines I send;
And if the cap should fit you too, my friend,
Ah, do not let it pass you idly by,
But put it on, and how it answers, try.
When the wild march of life I first began,
('Tis not so long ago) my earliest plan
Was just precisely what you now advise:
To eat, drink, laugh, sleep, wake, and thus grow wise.
From morn till eve, from eve till merry morn,
I kissed the rose, nor thought about the thorn.
My eye, my ear, my taste, I lived to please
In one unbroken round of idle ease.
Deep was my sleep beneath the magic spell,
And life went merry as a marriage bell.
On other objects soon my eyes were turned,
And Youth's romance within my bosom burned.
To dangle lightly by a lady's side,
And win a fav'ring look, was now my pride.
I cultivated graces, becks and smiles,
And sought preferment by such slavish wiles.
Amid the gambols of the thoughtless crowd,
My song and laugh were loudest of the loud.

But no! I see a Father's care,
Who works for me though unaware,
From greater ills Who fain would spare
                    My Mary.

So thou wert for a little given,
And from our arms then rudely riven,
Lest thou shouldst come 'tween me and Heaven,
                    My Mary!

The stiff quadrille and waltzer's smiling joy
Filled up the pleasures of the happy boy.
But sorrow gently pulled me by the sleeve,
And bade me wake and all my follies leave.
She told me that the worldling was a slave,
And all his treasure ended in his grave;
That beauty, honour, riches were but snares,
To catch the gaping dreamer unawares;
That handsome limbs and pockets richly lined
Will ne'er atone for a poor creeping mind;
That simpering lips and complimenting smile
May cover hateful passions all the while;
That they who get their good things here below
Shall drink the deepest of eternal woe.
She taught me, too, how Old Time scampers speedily,
And how to use his flying gifts most greedily;
She bade me hold the fellow by the heels,
And squeeze a blessing from each hour he steals;
She bade me leave the arms of leaden slumber,
And be afraid lest I the earth encumber.
Ah! shall I then despise the heavenly vision,
And treat the serious warning with derision?
Shall I despise the Liberty she gave,
And sell myself to earth again a slave?
No, Malcolm, no! You would not have it so!
E'en let me journey on then, as I go.

> My Saviour had an end in view,
> A nobler work for me to do;
> And He has something too for you,
>   My Mary!

Yet there could be no forgetting of one who had been, and would always be, singularly dear.

> Whene'er I bend my knee in prayer,
> And plead with Heaven to seek and spare,
> One name is all but foremost there –
>   'Tis Mary.

That was the boy's fancy, which was denied the boon it had sought. Seven years later, when he was making preparations in London for his journey to Palestine, there is this echo of the past: 'Rattled a long way to Manchester Street. Dined, and spent the evening with the Wettens. He a nice kind of man, very deaf; inquiring about divine things. Mary very little changed; not seemingly quite happy.' It is the last that we hear of her; but, in the list of those for whom he interceded with God, the first place, after his own immediate kinsfolk, is assigned to 'the MacGregors'.

There can be no harm in setting down the fact that, in the last five or six years of his life, McCheyne was twice engaged to be married. The details cannot be unravelled with lucidity and explicitness, for those who could have explained them unerringly, are no longer with us. But the fact appears to be indisputable.

About one of the engagements little can be recorded. Miss Maxwell was the daughter of a Dundee physician; and 'none named her but to praise'. At a later time she made a happy marriage with Colonel Bethune of Blebo; but it was the peculiar glory of her youth that she loved, and was loved by, this prince among the saints whose life-story we have been studying, 'one like to Christ so luminously'. The union between the two was not to be consummated. Her relatives, as some of their descendants believe, interposed to prevent it. They feared for that frail body of his, and judged it wiser that there should not be any wedding-bond. No precise times can be fixed for these events; but the time may have been 1837 or 1838.

In 1839, however, in a letter from Alexander Somerville, some suggestive sentences occur: 'I beg you will remember me with much affection both to your father and mother. I would say the same, if I dared, of a friend of yours' – and the word 'friend' is doubly underlined – 'but I suppose you would not allow me. I am dumb; but I sometimes hear of you (plural)'. The allusion now, in all probability, is to Miss Thain, of Heath Park, near Blairgowrie.[6]

The *Memoir and Remains* gives us three or four letters which McCheyne sent to the mother of this young lady, one of which was addressed to a brother who had died when he was a child, and one written to an older brother, then a student of divinity, and afterwards minister of the Free Church in New Machar.

The Thains lived for part of the year in Dundee, where they were adherents of St. Peter's congregation. They were greatly attached to its minister. It is proof of it that, before he started for the East, the mother told him of her double solici-

---

6. Mr. Thain was an elder, before the Disruption, in the parish church of Blairgowrie, and in his business was a shipowner in Dundee. When Mr. Macdonald and his people came over to the Free Church in 1843, it was Mr. Thain who gave them sail-cloth to cover the tent in which, for a time, they worshipped.

tude – the anxiety she felt for him, and the other anxiety, as keen and deep, for her own household in its loss of his teaching and help. 'Do be persuaded,' she said, 'to take care of yourself. We shall be often wandering with you in imagination when you are treading the ground our blessed Saviour trod. We shall look and long for your appearing again among us. May the Lord prosper your journey for His own glory and your good! Will you be so kind as to accept of the accompanying Bible as a small token of Christian regard! I should like that it be your pocket-companion during your travels, when I hope it may at times recall to your mind a family who, though absent in the flesh, shall be often with you in spirit, who earnestly desire an interest in your prayers, and who shall not cease to pray for you. Our cries are feeble; still I hope they shall reach the Throne, be heard and answered, through the merits and mediation of Him whom God heareth always. When far away in a land of strangers, will you remember my dear children? You know what is my heart's desire for them; help me in your prayers to God for them. I feel that almost the only thing I can do for them now is to pray, and sometimes I cannot even do that. I need grace to ask grace.'

We are interested in what follows: 'Poor Jessie has felt your absence all along very much;[7] and, now that it has come to this crisis, she is cast down. May she find that Jesus is ever near, though her Pastor is far away, who has so often gladdened her heart, when proclaiming redeeming love. She has been anxious to have a class in your Sabbath school, which Mr. Caird superintends. She feels that she is able to do very little, but should like much if she could be of any

---

7. It will be remembered that McCheyne was for some months in Edinburgh, before setting out on the mission to the Jews.

use in this way, while we are in town, which will be for some time yet.'

In Dr. Bonar's pages we are permitted to read the answer to this letter. 'I shall be quite delighted if Jessie is able to take a small part in the Sabbath school. She knows it is what I always told her – not to be a hearer of the Word only, but a doer. It is but a little time, and we shall work no more here for Him; O, that we might glorify Him on the earth!... Tell Jessie to stay herself upon God. Jesus continueth ever; He hath an unchangeable priesthood. Others are not suffered to continue by reason of death.'

A certain gravity, if not sombreness, hangs over the correspondence, alike on Mrs. Thain's side and on McCheyne's. They were a delicate family, these Thains, walking much in the solemn shadows of the other world, although by the tender mercy of our God they were freed from all disquieting dread of the shadows.

In January, 1842, little John Thain wrote, in a round and boyish hand, to his friend, staying then in the manse at Collace, that he might tell him, 'The Lord has thought it necessary to afflict me, to try and bring me to Himself'; that he might breathe out his ardent wish, 'O, may He make me one of His lambs'; and that he might ask the counsel and aid of one whom he fondly loved – 'It would make me very happy, if you would write me a letter, which I hope may do me good'. He had the letter for which he pleaded, and the richer comforts also of the Shepherd who gathers the lambs in His arm and carries them in His bosom; and then he went away to be with Christ.

His brother Alexander, whose very penmanship is modelled unconsciously but palpably upon that of McCheyne, and who would subscribe his letters from his student lodging in Rankeillor Street, in Edinburgh, 'Ever yours with all affection', survived, as we have seen, to enter the ministry; but he also ran his course with pathetic swiftness, and left the out-courts of the Temple soon for its Holy of Holies in the skies.

It may be, then, that the sister was not physically robust. The letters which passed between her and Robert McCheyne were destroyed by the friend into whose possession they came; perhaps it was best that curious eyes should have no chance of prying into such attachments and sanctities. There are no references, in anything written by relatives, to throw light on the problem why the engagement was protracted so long, and, when all was past and over, was deprived of its crown of marriage. Was it that her health, fragile and precarious like his own, forbade the union? Or, when his life closed somewhat suddenly at last, were they looking forward still to that wedlock which was not to be theirs? We only know that the ties which bound him to her and to the members of her family continued unbroken.

After his death Mrs. Thain wrote to his mother a letter overflowing with womanly sympathy, in which she wept the fullness from her own mind. 'My poor Alexander, he will be feeling deeply, having lost the best friend he had on earth. This is a house of weeping. Jessie is quite over-powered. She will write her dear friend Eliza as soon as she is able.'

But more significant still is the one letter that survives from Miss Thain herself. It belongs to the April of 1844, and was addressed to Eliza McCheyne after Robert's biography had appeared. 'You ask me what I think of the *Memoir and Remains*. Mr. Bonar kindly sent Mamma a copy. I began it the evening it came, and, as I could not rest until I had read it, finished the Memoir the next day. Although it seemed very, very precious, yet my first feelings were those of great regret – that it was so short, and thus the half has not been told. But as I had read it so hurriedly, and had only a confused idea of it, I am reading it over again, and enjoying it much more than the first time. It is fine indeed, most savoury; and don't you feel it very quickening, dear Eliza, to see what the dear subject of it attained to? O, to have such a sight of sin as he had, and to prize the Blood of sprinkling as he did! His great longing after holiness is a marked feature throughout the book, his desire being ever to be made "as holy as a pardoned sinner could be made".'

Then she reverts to her disappointment over the brevity of the record. 'Don't you think it was a pity to fill up the volumes with old publications, when there was so much new material? We have heard one or two say that they thought his friends would publish a third volume of letters. Have they any ground for saying so?' And yet, and yet, *the gold of that land is good; there is bdellium and the onyx stone*; and, 'O, I trust that the *Memoir* may be widely blessed!' Clearly, there was no slackening of the affection; and these two were husband and wife in spirit if not in actual experience.

But God, it would seem, wished him to remain a maiden knight, dedicated to Christ and eternity. He could not drink his fill at the springs of any human soul; he touched the earthly love close, then stood away. For Heaven was looking on him from its towers.

5

Indeed, the end of his battle had come. From his evangelistic tour in the North he returned to Dundee in the opening week of March. 'I am quite well,' he told Eliza. 'Every one declares I have turned fat on the expedition, and it is true. My heart was a little overworked and beat too hard; but nothing else was wrong.' It was, however, too roseate a diagnosis. On Sabbath, the 5th, he preached three times. All through the succeeding week he allowed himself no break in the crowd of his occupations.

On the following Sabbath he spoke in the forenoon, and again in the afternoon, to his own people; the afternoon text being found in that momentous question of the Epistle to the Romans, *What if God, willing to shew His wrath, and to make His power known, endured with much long-suffering the vessels of wrath fitted to destruction; and that He might make known the riches of His glory on the vessels of mercy, which He had afore prepared unto glory?* In the evening he rode to Broughty Ferry, taking with him a message which was gladsomer in its tone and less mysterious and awful, for now he preached from the heartening imperatives of Isaiah, *Arise, shine; for thy light is come.* These were his last texts; and they were symbolic of his entire ministry, in its consistent endeavour to do justice to all the varying aspects of revealed truth, the sovereignty as well as the grace, the terror no less than the consolation and the love, the winter and the summer both. To the very close God employed him to convey His own benedictions to hungry human hearts.

When death had called him away, a note was opened which the post had brought to the door during his illness. It was written by one who was a total stranger, to thank him for the hour of worship at Broughty Ferry. 'I heard you preach last Sabbath evening, and it pleased God to bless that sermon to my soul. It was not so much what you said, as your manner of speaking, that struck me. I saw in you a beauty in holiness that I never saw before.' Everything about McCheyne drew men Christward. More than most, he was the living epistle, signed with the King's autograph and sealed by His Spirit. It was with him as with young Sir Pelleas; they who met him wondered after him,

> ... because his face
> Shone like the countenance of a priest of old
> Against the flame about a sacrifice
> Kindled by fire from heaven.

On the Monday night there was a meeting in St. Peter's in connection with the ecclesiastical crisis. The Disruption had become unavoidable; and the office-bearers and members assembled to pledge themselves that, when the time came, they should cast in their lot with the Church of Scotland Free. Mr. Makgill Crichton spoke to them, and then their minister addressed them with an earnestness which lingered long in their recollection; they were not again to hear the voice which had meant so much to them in the past.

When the meeting was over, he was tired and unwell; but next day he was out once more, joining two of his people in marriage, Georgina Anderson and William Stewart. There is a story told of this service. A lady who was one of the guests was disposed to laugh at his manner as being affected. She sent a little girl across the room with a flower and a favour for him. The child ran up to him, saying in her baby prattle, 'Will 'oo put this in 'oor coat?' 'O yes, my dear,' he answered, 'but you must help me.' And so the child did, fastening the flower into his button-hole, and pinning the favour on his coat. 'Now,' he said, 'I have done what *you* wished; will you do what *I* would like?' 'Yes,' she replied. 'Well, I wish you to listen to the story of the Good Shepherd, who gave Himself for the sheep.' As he was talking, five or six other young people gathered round, pressing as near to him as they could; and he spoke as tellingly, as wooingly, as ever he had done from his pulpit. Then he turned to the friend who was afterwards to relate the incident, the Rev. Mr. McGillivray, and said, 'I must go; I feel such a pressure on my brow'. The fatal fever had set in; and the unpremeditated homily to the children was his very latest sermon. It was the lily-work on the top of his pillar.

Typhus was prevalent in the parish; and, since it never was his habit to screen and shield himself, he visited freely among the sick. It was almost inevitable that, worn as he was, he should catch the infection. At first the watchers round his bed clung to the expectation that he would recover. Here, for example, is a reassuring letter dispatched, on Thursday, the 16th of March, by Dr. Gibson, the beloved physician, to the parents waiting anxiously for tidings of the sufferer. 'I have no hesitation in writing you a few lines this evening, rejoiced as I am to say that he is, as I hoped he would be, greatly better already; – so much so that I have now little doubts of his being all right again in a very few days.' But soon things changed for the worse; and first the father and afterwards the mother crossed from Edinburgh to be with him.

Ere long he became unconscious; and, on Wednesday, the 22nd, there is a touching little note to Andrew Bonar from the sister who had served him so loyally and well. 'Dear friend, – If in your power, do come. It has pleased God to lay my beloved Brother on a sickbed from which there is little probability of his rising for many a day, should God spare him to us. The doctor says it is typhus fever, and this is the ninth day. He was perfectly sensible till this time yesterday, but had a bad night. Some hours he seemed to spend in prayer, in a low half-audible voice. Then he began to address his people so urgently that we could not bear to hear his dear voice, it was so moving. Today, for hours, he has talked about you, always thinking you were in the dining-room. "O, send him up to me! Send him up! Why will you keep him below?" Then he talked of Smyrna, and, indeed, is still at this moment speaking about you. O, come if you can!' Even in the delirium of illness he remained faithful to the human friend and the divine Master – faithful, also, to the souls who had been entrusted to his care.

It was the same to the last. Once he prayed, 'This parish, Lord! This people! This whole place!' At another time he took up Christ's petition and made it his own, 'Holy Father, keep through Thine own name those whom Thou hast given me'. Early on the morning of Saturday, March 25th, while Dr. Gibson stood beside him, he raised his hands as if to pronounce a benediction, and then let them fall. It was his way of going home. Again, we think of his Lord. *And it came to pass, while He blessed them, He parted from them, and was carried up into heaven.*

Robert McCheyne was not yet thirty years old, when he finished his course, and went to receive the crown of righteousness from the Judge, who was his Advocate and his Friend. There are some searching and incisive sentences that Professor Denney has written, which are in keeping here. He is commenting on St. Paul's phrase, *Your labour of love*, and he says: 'We have all been tired in our time, one may presume; we have toiled in business, or in some ambitious course, or in the perfecting of some accomplishment, or even in the mastery of some game or the pursuit of some amusement, till we were utterly wearied: how many of us have so toiled in love? How many of us have been wearied and worn with some labour to which we set ourselves for God's sake?

This is what the apostle has in view; and, strange as it may appear, it is one of the things for which he gives God thanks. But is he not right? Is it not a thing to evoke gratitude and joy, that God counts us worthy to be fellow-labourers with Him in the manifold works which love imposes?'[8]

McCheyne toiled in loving. This was his κόποV, his sedulous and continual travail, his labour. He tired himself, spent and exhausted himself, gave himself and all his powers away most willingly, for the glory of God and the good of men. And he had his task completed, when most of us are dreaming of commencing ours.

---

8. *The Epistles to the Thessalonians*, p. 29

CHAPTER 9

Aftermath

With much more force and truth than commonly attach to its use, one may quote of McCheyne the phrase, familiar as household words, which Tacitus employed of his father-in-law and hero, Cnaeus Julius Agricola, and may affirm of the minister of St. Peter's that he was *felix non vitae tantum claritate sed etiam opportunitate mortis* – happy not only in the radiancy of his life but in the moment of his death.

When God recalls His workers to their reward and to His own presence, 'He never is before His time and never is behind'; but surely there was a special fitness in the hour at which He bade this young soldier of His Son lay down his sword and enter into his rest. Had he lived to complete sixty or seventy years, he could not have accomplished more than he did, dying at twenty-nine; and his name and memory would have had less power to influence and subdue and compel. That he packed such saintliness and such service into so brief a span constituted Robert McCheyne's peculiar appeal to his own generation, and will always invest his example with an allurement and an impulse which are given to very few.

Three-quarters of a century after it happened, we can still feel the throb and pang of sorrow which his death occasioned. All Dundee was moved; and the day of his funeral was one of the greatest and most subduing in the annals of the city. Yielding to the importunities of the congregation, the father and mother consented that his body should be laid in the graveyard attached to the church whose name has been rendered famous and fragrant by his ministry, rather than in their own family burying-ground under the shadow of St. Cuthbert's spire in Edinburgh;[1] and the concourse in the streets was so dense, and the stillness that prevailed was so impressive, and the grief written on a thousand faces of old and young and rich and poor was so spontaneous and unrestrained, that Adam McCheyne said he understood why God had cut short so soon his son's life on earth – it was to prevent the townsfolk from making him their idol. It was not otherwise throughout Scotland, and beyond its boundaries, in Ireland to which he had gone more than once, and in different parts of England. The mourning was almost like that of Hadadrimmon in the valley of Megiddo, when all Judah and Jerusalem mourned for King Josiah. A statesman's death, or that of a prince of the realm, would hardly have been more profoundly felt.

It had, in not a few instances, the issue which he would

---

1. This was not done without some opposition on the part of friends; but Adam McCheyne displayed a fine temper. The Elders and Managers of St. Peter's had sent to him four resolutions, passed at a meeting held on Monday, March 27th. The third was in these terms: 'That it would be most gratifying to the feelings of this meeting, and in accordance with the wishes of the parishioners and congregation, that the remains of their beloved minister should be interred in the churchyard of St. Peter's – the spot to which in his discourses he so often pointed, and the place which will ever remain associated with his name and labours as a minister of Christ.' And this was the father's reply: 'I had determined to carry his poor remains with me to Edinburgh, to be interred with those of his family; but at your request I readily leave him with you. His name being in some degree associated with the town of Dundee, and more especially with the church and parish of St. Peter's, I see the propriety of your proposal, and acknowledge that for a soldier the most honourable grave is the field of battle.'

himself have most desired. It brought wayward hearts to God. The hushed voice, the torch which the eager runner had had to drop so quickly, affected them more than anything in his preaching or in his life. Some of the old people in St. Peter's would tell, years after he was gone, of a saying of his, 'When the boat has put off from the shore, you need not run. When should you run? *When the bell is ringing.*' There were many to whom the news of what had befallen, that Saturday morning of his departure, was like the ringing of the bell before the boat puts off from her moorings; at length they realized the need of running, if the favouring hour and the day of their salvation were not to be lost outright.

One story of this kind has a particular interest. In an early page of the *Memoir* some lines are preserved which he wrote to a young girl, related to him in a cousinly or half-cousinly way, who had said that 'she was determined to keep by the world'; they are lines the colours of which are dark, ominous, and alarming, 'as when some painter dips his pencil in the gloom of earthquake and eclipse':

> She has chosen the world,
>   And its paltry crowd;
> She has chosen the world,
>   And an endless shroud...!
> But Bethlehem's star
>   Is not in her view;
> And her aim is far
>   From the harbour true.

More than once, in those days of his own first love, he had laid siege, on behalf of his Master Christ, to Constance Bullen's soul. These verses also, belong to the spring of 1832:

How lovely the tints of the butterfly's wing!
      How gaily it flutters along!
It pleases my eye, and its praises I sing,
      But my love is as light as the song.

The hues of the rainbow oft dazzle my eyes,
      And my bosom expands at the view;
But the false fleeting vision deceives me and flies,
      And my love for it vanishes too.

Ah, Constance inconstant! how long? ah, how long
      Wilt thou flutter existence away?
The love that's worth having can never belong
      To the heart that but loves for a day.

Go, ask of the butterfly, who are its friends,
      And where is its sheltering bower,
When the pitiless storm on the garden descends,
      And the beauty is stripped from the flower.

In mirth and in madness it revels today,
      But seek for its glory tomorrow;
In the cold breath of night it has withered away,
      It has vanished in darkness and sorrow.

And so may the lovely and mirth-loving thing,
      That waltzes through life's giddy day,
Be gazed at and praised like the butterfly's wing,
      Then languish and wither away.

Though loud is the laugh of the flickering throng,
      And the smile from each bright face is beaming,
Their laughter shall turn into weeping ere long,
      And the smile be the smile but of seeming.

Ah, list then, my Constance, the well-meaning strain,
   Nor bid the intruder begone!
I offer no vows, for my labour were vain,
   And Truth is the goddess I own.

Away from the halls of the false-hearted crew
   Dwells peaceful contentment of mind:
Her taper burns steady, her loving is true,
   No flattery with her shall you find.

But for eleven years, although the admonitory words pursued her, and broke in upon the quiet of conscience every little while, she persisted in preferring the shows to the substance and the tinsel above the fine gold. Then came the unexpected shock and summons of his death. And at last he won his victory, and she surrendered to his Lord. Long afterwards, at a Mildmay Conference, in June, 1876, she drew Dr. Bonar aside and told him the history, adding that she had a son in the army who was Christ's follower too. Race unto race rises up to call McCheyne blessed.

No one in the communion of all saints owes a larger debt to his biographer. The *Memoir and Remains* is an undying spiritual classic; and it has travelled round the circuit of the world. When the centenary of its author was celebrated in the summer of 1910, Dr. James Wells wrote to the newspapers that 'about two hundred thousand copies had been sold in our country', and that 'some twenty years ago' more than that number had already been sold in America. Including translations into other languages, he estimated that not less than half a million copies were in circulation at the moment when his letter was penned. Yet Andrew Bonar used to tell how wonderfully glad he was when he found a publisher for the book, and how his biggest hopes for it at the outset of its career had been that an edition of two thousand copies might find purchasers and readers.

It is one of those elect books through which God has wrought His conquering miracles of grace. Power has emanated from it to reverse the trend and current of human lives. The love of Christ has leaped from its chapters and pages, to capture men and women, and to bind them to their Healer and their King in the bondage which is liberty and delight.

Over in Ireland, some time after the awakening of 1859, Mr. Lyon of Broughty Ferry overheard, in the streets of Carrickfergus, a mother calling to her boy, 'Robert! Robert McCheyne!' He discovered that, when she feared and quaked exceedingly under the thunders and lightnings of the Mount of the Law, it was the reading of the *Memoir* which had brought her peace; and, in grateful remembrance of her burden lost and her emancipation won, she gave McCheyne's name to her child.

One Lord's Day, Mr. Wilson of Abernyte was preaching in St. Peter's, and an American gentleman came to speak to him when the service closed. 'I was converted,' he said, 'through the *Memoir* of McCheyne, and I resolved that my first Sabbath in Europe should be spent in his church.'

In the Highlands of Scotland, a farm-servant, a slave to the lust for strong drink, and the terror of the neighbourhood, was running unchecked his evil way. But God, whose rod comforts as well as His staff, had compassion on him, and laid him down under a serious illness. Reaching over to the window-sill, where some books were lying, he took up a copy of McCheyne's *Memoir*. Before he had read far, the Holy Spirit convicted him of his great sinfulness; and then his distress was sore and deep. But he persevered with his reading; and soon the book which had smitten taught him

the secret of abiding health in the redemption of Jesus Christ:
it resembled the sword of the Cid which wounded in order to
recover and cure.

Looking in at a shop window, a young English clergyman
– he was Canon Woodward of Liverpool in subsequent years
– saw flattened against the glass the front page of the *Memoir*, with the portrait and the signature, 'Yours till glory'. It
seemed to him a quaint and extraordinary mode of subscribing oneself, and he went in and bought the volume; and it
'enticed him home to be forgiven'.

In a ship which was wrecked off Cape Agulhas were a
working woman and her husband. They were brought ashore;
but they had lost everything except their copy of the *Memoir*. 'I would not part with it,' the woman said. 'I can get
another Bible, even in a heathen land, but not another Mc-
Cheyne!'

These are but samples of a hundred similar tales of succour and salvation, which cluster round this accusing and
vivifying and upbuilding biography. And what an immortality Robert McCheyne has had!

Two months after his death, the Disruption of the Scottish Church was an accomplished fact. Writing to Collace
on the 24th of May, young Alexander Gatherer, who was in
temporary charge of the parish of St. Peter's, had this to say
to Mr. Bonar: 'The dark days predicted so frequently by our
friend seem now at hand. How much he would have enjoyed
them! How delighted he would have been with the proceed-
ings of last Thursday! I recollect, in writing from the Convocation with such a prospect in view, he said, "How happy it
is to live at such a time!"'

The darkness, to McCheyne's thinking, was shot through
and through with lambent flames of hope; if it was night, it

was a night of stars; and a noble sunrise was at hand. The
Disruption was more than the assertion of the Church's independence from the interference and control of the State; it
was a signal and enriching spiritual movement.

The years of preparation which led up to it had witnessed
the resurgence throughout Scotland of evangelical religion;
and it was in the atmosphere of this new-born personal religion that the Free Church started on its course. McCheyne
and William Burns had been among God's chief instruments
in producing the quickening generation. While Chalmers and
Cunningham and Candlish were fighting in the high places
of the field for the freedom of the Kirk, they sought to awaken
the individual soul from slumber into concern, to teach it the
meaning of repentance and faith, and to persuade it to embrace without delay the sufficient Saviour who is offered to
it in the gospel. By the presence and help of Him whose they
were and whom they served, they were marvellously suc-
cessful.

The Church of 1843, and the years that followed, was
rooted and grounded not merely in an inveterate distrust of
Erastianism, but in an intense love for the Lord Jesus Christ;
and, if both soils are good, the latter is, beyond question, the
better of the two. That this best love of all had such regnancy
and compelling force was due, under God from whom all
blessings flow, to Robert McCheyne as much as to any of
the Church's spokesmen and sons.

It was another world from that of 'Jupiter' Carlyle, and
we find it difficult to believe that the redoubtable minister of
Inveresk was not yet forty years in his grave; must it not be
an altogether measureless virtue which resides in the simple
and urgent proclamation of the gospel, and in the holy life
that is the best commentary on the gospel's truth and power?

For many reasons McCheyne transcends Alexander Carlyle, as high as heaven is above the earth.

To begin with, there was the substance of his message. Here were no discussions of rudimentary moralities, no adventures in political economy and essays in criticism, no hints of how to behave in polite society. Here was the direct vision of the eternal realities; the sense that nothing can be so momentous as sin, and salvation, and the atoning Cross of Christ, and the trust of the helpless heart in Him who died and rose again; the definite transacting with guilt-laden men on behalf of a God whose righteousness is unbending, yet whose name is Love, and who wills not that one of them should perish; the refusal to be satisfied until every argument and persuasion and solicitation have been tried which will humble the proud will, and startle the sleeping conscience, and heal the wounded spirit, and lead the wanderers home.

Then there was the manner of the messenger. In the pulpit, as out of it, the Moderates were men of the world, careful to display their *savoir faire*, guiding language and gesture and demeanour by regard for the conventions and proprieties, compact of decorum and dignity. They were not bowed into reverence. They did not tremble beneath the awful responsibility and the sacred privilege of bearing the burden of the Lord. It was not a constant personal amazement to them that they should have been chosen to publish the word of reconciliation.

But to McCheyne it was always an amazement. 'Andrew Bonar,' Dr. J. H. Jowett has recently written, 'has told us with what full and delicate wonder Robert McCheyne carried his ministry in the Lord. In their conversation he would frequently break out into deep and joyful surprise. The glory of his vocation irradiated common duty like a halo, and God's statutes became his songs'.[2] Is it not the true attitude, the seemly comportment? And, behind the message, there was the man, so cleansed from self and sin, so enamoured of Christ. 'He was the meekest, calmest, and holiest believer that ever I saw,' one who knew him wrote to his mother.

From Morar a Highland laird, who was Roman Catholic in faith, Aeneas Ronald Macdonell, bore the same testimony in an ingenuous accent of his own. 'I only once, and that but for a very short time, enjoyed the company of your dear departed Robert, yet I can honestly declare that I was never so much prepossessed in favour of any one. And when I heard his fervent eloquence in the pulpit, the candour and sincerity of his discourse so plainly spoke the piety of his heart that I could not help saying to myself, "That man is booked for Heaven!"' 'Assuredly' – it is Dr. Candlish's tribute – 'he had more of the mind of his Master than almost any one I ever knew, and realized to me more of the likeness of the beloved disciple.'

For a final delineation of the priestly and constraining character, let us hearken to his friend, James Hamilton of Regent Square. We can imagine nothing more beautiful and more adequate than his letter to Adam McCheyne.

'This is the most solemn event which has happened since I became a minister. It has made the last two days, days of darkness and gloominess. For besides your loss and his people's, and the loss to us who loved him as a brother, it is a heavy stroke to the Church and land.

'The removal of so bright a light at such a time, is a righteous but terrible judgment. I do not wish to lose the person in the public warning; for I feel that I greatly needed it. Indolence and levity and unfaithfulness are sins that beset me;

2. *The Preacher: his Life and Work*, pp. 17, 18.

and his living presence was a rebuke to all these, for I never knew one so instant in season and out of season, so impressed with the invisible realities, and so faithful in reproving sin and witnessing for Christ. His feeble frame made his labours the more wonderful, and his sensitive spirit made fidelity more difficult to him than it would have been to a mind less tender. Love to Christ was the great secret of all his devotion and consistency; and, since the days of Samuel Rutherfurd, I question if the Church of Scotland has contained a more seraphic mind, one that was in such a constant flame of love and adoration toward *Him that liveth and was dead.*

'His continual communion with God gave wonderful sacredness to his character; and, during the week that he spent with us last November, it seemed as if there were a sanctity diffused through our dwelling. That visit was useful to many; and his Sabbath evening sermon on "Following the Lord fully" made a deep impression then, which the tidings of last Monday have revived in new solemnity. We feel now what a kind Providence it was, which led us to ask that visit and induced him to comply.

'On the Friday evening I accompanied him to the railway station. He was anxious to get a seat in an empty carriage, that he might have undisturbed leisure for meditation and prayer; but in this he was disappointed, for another passenger came in ...

'Since Monday morning, he has been the one thought present to my mind; and, now that I am writing to you, I find a mournful pleasure in recalling those solemn days in St. Peter's, and those hallowed evenings in his own house, which can never return; as I trust the beauties of holiness which I then saw in him may be profitable lessons and motives all my life henceforward.

'I doubt not, my dear Sir, that the Holy Spirit, the Comforter, will sanctify to you and yours this heavy trial. Seldom has a weeping family so many prayers offered in their behalf. May you yet, in the immeasurably larger supply of *His* presence, find it *expedient for you* that the desire of your eyes has *gone away*. My tongue is not learned like his, else I would try to speak a word in season in this hour of sorrow. But you have no need of earthly comfort. Our own *night cometh*, and then *the morning cometh*, and, when He Himself is come, sorrow shall flee away.'

'Since the days of Samuel Rutherfurd the Church of Scotland has not contained a more seraphic mind' – that is the right estimate and the fitting word.[3]

We have reached the close of the history that has so little in it and so much, whose wealth and fruit are known to Christ alone. We have seen how Robert McCheyne did his part in breaking up the long frost and in bringing in the spring of the year; and not the promise of spring simply, but the warmth

---

3. To James Hamilton's pen-portrait it is worthwhile adding Robert Macdonald's, then of Blairgowrie, afterwards of North Leith. 'I remember, one of the earliest visits I paid to London, I was going up to Mr. Nisbet's shop, as he and another gentleman were coming out. Mr. Nisbet said to the other, "This is a friend of Mr. McCheyne's." The gentleman at once took hold of me, and said, "Did you know that remarkable man?" "Yes," I said, "he was an intimate friend of mine." "What do you think," he went on, "was the secret of that man's holiness?" and, without waiting, he answered his own question: "Don't you think it was *watchfulness*?"

'I think he was right, the more I consider it. Often he was with me at the manse in Blairgowrie, and he always left a benediction behind him. He was always on his guard. My old Adam would have been almost glad

of summer and the abundance of harvest. *Lo, the winter is past, the rain is over and gone, the flowers appear on the earth, the time of the singing of birds is come, and the voice of the turtle is heard in our land.*

But today, we have journeyed far since that March of 1843, when he laid down his ministry. Scottish religion, as we know it, has not the same note of passion, of stress, and of immediacy which rang through the words he spoke and the life he lived. The evil of sin, and the certainty and the anguish of his wage, do not oppress us as much as they oppressed him; nor are we so captivated by the redemption prepared and finished for guilty men on the Cross of Our Lord and Saviour Jesus Christ.

It is not that we deny these central truths; it is rather that they have ceased to dominate us as imperiously as they dominated the preachers of the older generation, till they were weary with forbearing, and besought men in Christ's stead to be reconciled to God, and went out to the highways and hedges to compel their brothers to come in to the supper of the King's Son. The Biblical scholarship of our time is in advance of theirs; we have access to enviable stores of learning of which they knew little. The mind does its full share in

---

to see a slip, I forgot so many things myself. This was his characteristic, *If a man purge himself... he shall be a vessel unto honour*. We often lose golden opportunities by not being usable. Mr. McCheyne's holiness was noticeable even before he spoke a word; his appearance spoke for him. There was a minister in the north of Scotland with whom he spent a night. He was so marvellously struck by this about him, that when Mr. McCheyne left the room, he burst into tears, and said, "O, that is the most Jesus-like man I ever saw". Robert McCheyne would sometimes say but one word, or quote a text; but it was blessed. I never got even a note from him that I could burn. There was always something in it worth keeping; God seemed to bless all he wrote.'

our presentation of the gospel; but perhaps there is less of
heart than there used to be, so that we do not baptize our
work as our fathers did theirs, in intercession and in tears.

A few months back, a citizen of Dundee, walking along a
quiet street, saw chalked on a pillar the two words, 'Alas,
McCheyne!' They were not only the *desiderium tam cari
capitis*; they were – so at least the onlooker read them – the
lamentation of a regretful and orphaned soul over a new age
separated from its predecessor in thought and temper, in aim
and spirit. Yet there is no need for pessimism, and despond-
ency would be unpardonable. The Moderatism of the eighteenth century is hopelessly discredited; and, under the
surface, the religion of Scotland still beats true to the Evangelicalism which defeated it and drove it from the field.

There are tokens, moreover, of coming revival, an expect-
ancy in the air, a conviction not to be suppressed that God
will soon revisit His people, fulfilling amongst them His
former signs and greater signs than those. The fire which
has been burning in our world ever since Pentecost is not
extinguished, and cannot be; its strength will be revealed
again, and we shall warm our hands and hearts at it. *Unto
you that fear My name*, God says, *shall the Sun of Righteousness arise with healing in His wings*.

When this fresh morning dawns, the men and women who
publish His tidings will be a great host. They will not couch
their message in McCheyne's dialect. They will not repro-
duce his style. But they will reassert in its essential ingredients the gospel in which he gloried. They will feel themselves,
as perpetually he felt himself, in the awful and blessed presence of God. And they will wear, like him, the Christly dress,
the fine linen clean and white which is the righteousness of
the saints.

INDEX

EXTRACTS FROM THE
DIARY OF JESSIE THAIN

Let me in a few words explain how this Diary came into my hands. The late Mr William MacFarquhar, Dingwall, Ross-shire, once purchased some theological books. Among them was found Jessie Thain's Diary. There was no name to indicate who the original owner of the books was. After Mr MacFarquhar's death the Diary became the prized possession of his daughter, Miss Helen A MacFarquhar. It was left to the Rev Duncan MacLachlan, Maryburgh, to transcribe its contents. This he did for his own private enjoyment. Mr MacLachlan was kind enough to let me use his copy. It was our desire that the original manuscript should be left untouched and unmarked. Both Miss MacFarquhar and he were happy at the suggestion of printing these extracts. We felt that it was not in vain that God had so long preserved this precious fragment of spiritual autobiography from the pen of one of His children.

Murdoch Campbell
Resolis, Conon Bridge,
Ross-shire,
September 1955

31st December, 1843

I have often intended to note down things of interest to me; but have through much procrastination, never yet fulfilled my intention. I would now wish to do so, that I may not forget my own multiplied evil doings, or the manifold mercies of the Lord. I would be humbled in the dust because of my continual backsliding, and would also praise God for restoring my soul and for fulfilling that sweet promise, 'I will heal their backsliding; I will love them freely'. Oh that I may never open my mouth any more because of my shame, seeing the Lord is at peace with me notwithstanding all that I have done against Him. Well may it be said, 'Who is a God like unto Thee, that pardoneth iniquity, and passeth by the transgression of the remnant of His heritage?' The Lord grant that whatever is recorded here may be faithfully done, according to His own blessed mind and will, and that all may be to His glory through Jesus Christ our Lord.

This day was privileged to partake of the Lord's Supper, which was dispensed in Rattray Free Church for the first time. Although it is but a month since I was permitted to sit at His Table with my much loved friend, Eliza McCheyne, by my side, yet again have I had the opportunity of celebrating this the sweetest and most solemn of all the ordinances, and thus suitably closing this year. 'Bless the Lord, O my soul, and forget not all His benefits.' Many were the precious truths declared this day, and I cannot but hope it was to not a few, a time of refreshing from the presence of the Lord. Although I *did* enjoy it, yet not so much as I might have done, doubtless on account of my own lifelessness. A most suitable and powerful sermon was preached from the words, 'Worthy is the Lamb'. The first Table service was sweet on the words, 'Fear not, I know ye seek Jesus that was cruci-

fied. He is not here; he is risen, as he said...' The preacher
said God was to be thanked for an empty tomb and an occupied Throne, and for thus speaking to believers of *their* death.
They do not know what circumstances they may be in at that
solemn hour; whether a gentle and loved voice shall whisper
to them a promise of God's word, and a kindly and loved
hand close their eyelids; or whether they shall end their days
among strangers. But Jesus knows the time, place, and manner of their death. 'My times are in Thy hand', and they could
not be in better hands. Their death might come by a stroke,
or they might die, as it were, by inches; but although it did
come by a stroke, a sting could not come along with it; for
Jesus had laid bare His own bosom to receive the sting, so
that believers were assured there could be no sting nor curse
in their death. They should be comforted by looking upon
their own death in the glass of Christ's death.

From the deadness of my affections, and unpreparedness
of my heart, felt most uncomfortable about going to the
Table. I felt, as I have often done before, how great is the
guilt of God's own children, and how much deeper my sins
are since believing than what they were before that time. I
felt I had not rightly fulfilled the injunction, 'Let a man examine himself and so let him eat of this bread and drink of
this cup'. Remembering with trembling that word, 'For this
cause many are weak and sickly among you and many sleep',
I thought that I should not go, less in judgment I might die at
the Table. And yet I thought I could not stay away, for I felt
that if I had never accepted Jesus before, I was willing to do
so at that moment.

When stepping forward to the Table, I was comforted by
these words coming forcibly to my mind, 'Fear not for I have
redeemed thee, I have called thee by thy name, thou art mine'.

And also, 'The Lord will not cast off those whom He hath chosen'. Although lifeless at the Table, yet felt more peaceful than I expected, and snatched at a few sentences spoken to those who were doubting whether they were the Lord's people or not. Felt as if they were addressed to myself. 'Are you saying in yourself at this moment, "I am vile"? Do you account Christ precious? Do you look upon prayer as a privilege?' to all which I thought my heart answered 'Yes'; and so was gladdened thereby. Again I felt how true it is that if any were chosen and loved, it was all of sovereign grace, and because the Lord loved them; for, 'He hath mercy on whom He will have mercy'. He has done this that the redeemed through all eternity might be saying, 'by the grace of God I am what I am'.

Besought the Lord to pardon all my past iniquity, especially my sin of idolatry in loving the creature more than the Creator, and to enable me to say from the heart, 'What have I to do any more with idols?' and 'Whom have I in heaven but Thee, and there is none upon all the earth that I would desire besides Thee'. Asked for grace to lay aside every weight and the sin which doth so easily beset me, that I might run with patience the race that is set before me looking unto Jesus. Resolved to stir up myself to lay hold on God, and to endeavour to be more spiritually minded.

O Lord save me from having nothing more than sleepy desires, and grant that these resolutions may not be like many in days gone by, made only to be broken. Although I can do nothing in my own strength, let me ever remember that I must not sit still, but labour to enter into that rest. Endeavoured to enter anew in covenant with the Lord and to give myself to Him, beseeching Him that however heartlessly I, at that moment, did my part, that He would take my body, soul and spirit, mind, will and affections, all that I am and mould me according to His own mind and will. Again I earnestly prayed Him to open up to me a door of usefulness – a way whereby I may serve Him, living no longer unto myself but unto Him who died for me and rose again.

Monday evening, 1st January, 1844

I did not go out last evening, but I hear Mr Baxter preached an excellent sermon from that wonderful verse, 'Father, I will that they also whom Thou hast given Me, be with Me where I am; that they may behold my glory, which Thou hast given Me; for Thou lovedst Me before the foundation of the world'. Well do I remember the time when I heard Mr Baxter on these words. It was on the last Sabbath that Eliza McCheyne and I were in St Peter's, on which day we were there together – a day which shall not soon be forgotten.

Felt happier today than yesterday. Was somewhat thankful and able to praise the Lord for all His mercies. I do not know what may be before me in this year, but Oh may the Lord enable me to think, speak and act, to read and pray differently from what I have ever done before. But O how I have sinned against Him this day already. I can only go again to the blood of Jesus Christ His Son that cleanseth from all sin. 'Unto whom can I go but unto Thee, Thou alone hast the words of eternal life.' Where can I flee but unto Him from Whom I have so deeply revolted?

Was gladdened this morning by a long kind letter from dear Eliza McCheyne. May all her desires for me return tenfold into her bosom. Heard Mr Bain preach this evening, a lively, comforting and solemn sermon from the words, 'The night is far spent, the day is at hand'. Although I do in some measure, feel this to be a night of darkness and ignorance; a night of sorrow and affliction; a night of doubts and fears; yet I surely do not feel it as I might, else I would be longing more for the day which will be bright and cloudless; blissful and glorious; the day which will be eternal and unchangeable.

Although I have met in the year that is past, with what has cost me many a sorrowful hour, yet how much is there of cleaving to the dust – how little of a desire to depart and be with Christ, which is far better.

14th January

Went to the school last Sabbath evening. Was very weary on returning home, but thankful that I had been able to go. Oh that the Lord may use me as the weak instrument of lasting good to the souls of these dear children – to those of them whom He may have already saved, and to those (the greater part of them) who are still thoughtless and careless about divine things. Read to the girls a long letter from Alexander[1] to themselves. They listened attentively and a few seemed affected. Oh that it may have been blessed to them!

Not having been very well I remained at home this forenoon, that I might be able for the afternoon and evening, but alas how little am I in the Spirit on the Lord's Day. Instead of entering into God's rest, which they who have believed ought to do (especially on the day of rest), I am grovelling among the things of earth. Instead of sitting with Christ in heavenly places, my soul cleaves to the dust. The Lord pardon my constant neglect of the commandment 'Remember the Sabbath day to keep it holy'.

---

1. Her brother, Alexander Thain, who afterwards became minister of the Free Church.

Thursday, 18th January

I heard last Saturday from dear Isabella Williamson of her intended union with Mr Moncur. O! that this step may be of the Lord, and prove for her good and His Glory. Tuesday last brought some things to my remembrance – *being a year that day since our dear friend[1] was here, and whom we then saw for the last time.* How ignorant we are of what a day will bring forth, for how little did I then dream that I was not to see his dear face again till the Lord Jesus shall come and all His saints with Him. May I be gladdened by the thought of the next time I hope to see him. Oh that our next meeting may be at the right hand of Jesus – when I trust to be part of His crown of joy and rejoicing in the Lord. And may I continually offer up what he did when last I saw him – '*May all, O Lord, we think and do and say be sprinkled with blood, and be pleasing in thine eyes.*'

Tuesday evening, 23rd January

Attended last week at this time the children's meeting at Couper. After tea and anecdotes from the ministers in the hall, we all adjourned to the church, where the children were addressed in a most solemn manner by Mr Andrew Bonar on the necessity of their coming to Christ, and that for three reasons:

1st - Because their danger was very real;

2nd - Because their sins were very great, and

3rd - Because Christ was willing to receive them.

Mr Archibald Ferguson then spoke to them, in a weighty manner, on the danger of delaying to come to Jesus, illustrating his theme by the case of the old and young women who were drowned because they adhered to Christ. He

---

1. R. M. McCheyne

showed the children that they were all condemned to die, and that the waves of God's wrath would come further and further upon them until they went over their heads. He urged them to flee to the King for pardon, for delay was dangerous. Perhaps they would say that they could not run; that as the women were tied to the stake so they were bound by sin; but if they could not run they could cry, and the Lord hears all who really cry to Him. If they were offered a rich present, a gold guinea, or a fine dress, they would not wait until they were old. So they should go immediately to Jesus who has unsearchable riches, gold tried in the fire, and a beautiful robe to give them. They cannot have better company than Christ's in their journey through the world; and they cannot have a better guide than the Lord. They cannot have a better home than Heaven. And although the road seems rough, yet if they are brought to that land, they would be willing to go over the same way again to get to such a sweet Home at the end. Therefore, they must come to Christ now. They should offer up that great prayer, 'O satisfy us *early* with Thy mercy that we may rejoice and be glad in Thee all our days'. Some think that religion is a gloomy thing, but Moses was a wiser man than any of us and he said, '*Satisfy* us early with Thy mercy'. Yes, if you come to Christ you will never repent it. You are young just now, but although you live long you will never meet with any who were sorry they came so soon to Jesus. You will meet with many who were sorry they did not come sooner. May the Lord (Mr Ferguson said) find you, and enable you to find Him.

Mr Gillies then addressed them on the necessity of a new heart, and Christ's willingness to give it to them. Shewed them that as it is by a watch's mainspring that it is regulated, so it is the state of their hearts that guides their life. God has said that the heart is wicked by nature, and therefore it must be true. As a crab apple tree will never of itself bear a living or Ribston pippin, so unless they got a new heart they could never lead a new life. He told them they would never be happy until they were holy, and that they would never get to heaven until they were holy. As a goldfish is out of its element when not in water so if the devil or the unregenerate got into heaven, they would wish to leave it. Christ was willing to give them a new heart, and they should plead that promise, 'A new heart also will I give you'.

Mr Cook then spoke on the importance of Sabbath school instruction, chiefly with regard to its beneficial effects on the domestic circle, and on the congregation which he illustrated by a case of some that came under his own observation.

Mr Moncur then addressed the parents. He said there might be some parents present who were happy in looking upon their children, and this was well. There might be others who had none to look upon because their children were in the grave. There might be others who were looking upon their children and who would have no children to look upon by that time next year. He would be glad if his remarks had the effect of making even one parent erect a family altar to God. He reminded them they would never all meet again in the same circumstances, and urged them to go home and pray.

Mr Bain then shortly addressed the teachers. He wished them to be impressed with the thought of having immortal souls to teach for eternity. They should bring every case to God. To the children he said how sad it would be after they had heard from so many ministers if anyone went away without Christ. They needed God's Spirit that all that they had heard might be blessed to them. How happy he would be if they were saying what a little girl said when listening to a sermon, that she would love to be one of Christ's lambs. Mr Bain closed by speaking of our all meeting one day at the Throne of God.

Thursday, 25th January

At the school last Sabbath evening read to the girls (at their own request) Alexander's letter a second time, which, the Lord grant, may come to them as a message of power from Himself. Dear Isabella Williamson heard the half of the class, and I think I was enabled to teach them with more liberty and comfort than usual. When finished, I felt amazed, considering my sin and sloth, at the Lord's great goodness and tender mercy. But, Oh, I have a wicked heart and there is a tempting devil; for the thought just came to mind that it was perhaps by chance that I was enabled to speak to them and that it was not the Lord who had given me freedom to speak. But immediately I said within myself, 'Get thee behind me, Satan'. I endeavoured to ask the Lord to pardon me because of this thing. 'Rejoice not against me, O mine enemy, when I fall I shall arise.' Oh that I may be more watchful in the time to come; and that the Lord would bruise Satan under my feet shortly.

Liked Mr Cook's lecture in the afternoon of Sabbath on the 15th Psalm. His remarks on 'he that worketh righteousness' were very good. The life of Christ within us buds in acts of service, and in refraining from raising or receiving an evil report which would injure our neighbour's good name. Likewise on that part as to our honouring 'them that fear the Lord', he dwelt on the close union that subsists between all the brethren of Christ. He spoke solemnly on 'he that sweareth to his own hurt'. Those there are who take an oath, promising to be the Lord's at the Communion Table, and who then break their engagement.

I thought what he said on this Psalm came with a different power to anything I had heard from him, and it seems he was ill-prepared and felt his own weakness so much that he was afraid to open his mouth. This is just another proof that the Lord is the strength of His servants. He gives them words to speak, and when they cast themselves upon Him, perfects His strength in their weakness.

Saturday evening, 3rd February
Had Mr Archibald Ferguson with us a few days ago. He exchanged with Mr Cook last Sabbath. It was an interesting day, for he is a wonderful preacher. Never heard him preach before except on the evening of last Thursday in Mr Gillies' church. His text was, 'And Peter followed afar off'. He showed:

1st - That natural principles and resolutions are unable to bind us to the Saviour.

2nd - That a decay in the soul is gradual.

3rd - That a backsliding state is dangerous and deceitful.

The sermon was very striking and solemn, and the descriptive parts very fine. Last Sabbath was still better, more powerful, and manifesting great knowledge of the Bible, and a searching into the mine of wealth that is to be found there. How I wish that I could remember more. Not being yet accustomed to his style is, I think, partly the reason why I don't recollect his sermon better. He uses so many similitudes, and his style is clear. He lectured on Luke 9, verses 51, 52, 53, was very instructive. Began by speaking of the Tabernacle in the wilderness with the cloud of glory resting upon it, as being a type of the human body of Christ; and as it was taken over to Canaan so was He received up into Glory.

He said a great deal on, 'And when the time was come' – when the hour had struck. Spoke of the place He was going to – Jerusalem, and of the manner in which He went – 'He steadfastly set His face'. He might easily have slain the men who reeled back when He said, 'I am He'. The same power that healed Malchus' ear might have destroyed them, but love was the cord that bound Jesus to the Cross. But why go to Jerusalem? When the type (the scapegoat) was sent into the desolations of the wilderness, why does Jesus go to Jerusalem? Because, what could be more a wilderness to Him than the crowded city? What could be such a wilderness to Him as the palace of the high priest?

'And sent messengers before his face.' These words show the divinity of Christ, that He could command attendants whensoever He pleased. The poor Carpenter when walking by the Sea of Galilee could, by saying, 'Follow Me', make men leave their work and their kindred and follow Him whithersoever He went. The ties of nature and affection give way before the drawing grace of Christ. His servants are but messengers. They only tell what has been told them and they are not true to their Lord if they fail to deliver His word faithfully.

'Before His face.' Jesus comes up after them. The steps of their Master are heard behind them.

'To make ready for Him.' Their first care was to provide for Him. This should be the highest aim of ministers. It is the most blessed point for them to reach – to desire above all things the glory of their Master. This can only happen when they say with John, 'I must decrease but He must increase'.

'And they did not receive Him.' In this they showed cruelty, folly and ignorance; cruelty in as much as it was against all the rules of kindness and hospitality not to give Him refreshment on His way; folly and ignorance, for some have entertained angels unawares. Jesus would have amply repaid them for what He cost them, and would very likely have given them the better blessings of His grace, even the bread of life.

'Because His face was as though He would go to Jerusalem.' They would not receive Him because He had passed Mount Gerizim (which it seems evident from what the woman at the well said to Jesus, as well as from other parts, was where the Samaritans worshipped) and was going on to Jerusalem, thus showing them His contempt of their false worship.

Learn from all this three things:

1st -   Christ's willingness to die for His people. No one could have obliged Him to suffer, but He said, 'Lo, I come, in the volume of the book it is written of me'.

2nd - That you may be guilty of rejecting Christ although you have never seen Him. It is probable that Jesus himself did not go into this village; but His messengers were refused in His name. If we reject the messengers of Christ whether they come to us in His ministry, His providence or His word, He counts it all the same as if we rejected Himself.

3rd - *Are there not many villages of Samaritans in our days*? Do you say you have no room for Jesus? I answer you have room for the world, room for lusts, room for sin, in short, room for anything except the weary Traveller from Galilee. Is it because it would be costly that you do not receive Him? Well, it may cost you a right hand or a right eye, but Jesus will amply repay you. He is a debtor to no man. He will give an hundredfold here with persecutions and in the world to come life everlasting. Is it idolatry that is making us reject Him? Are we clinging to our idols? Well, if we receive Him, He will bring us to something better than Mount Gerizim – He will lead us to Mount Zion.

Tuesday, 6th

On the afternoon of Sabbath, the 28th, Mr Ferguson preached a sweet and comforting sermon from, 'Be it unto thee even as thou wilt'. I grieve that I remember so little of it, but will put down what I recollect; in order that that little may not be forgotten. He began by saying that God is no stinted Benefactor, He opens His hand liberally and pours down blessings. He acts like a Sovereign. He maketh His sun to shine on the evil and on the good. He is not like the merchant who weighs out the commodity in proportion to what he is to be paid for it. Indeed if God uses the balances at all, it is to weigh out the trials His people need; it is to see how little affliction they will require. But it is more apparent that God acts as a sovereign because *He gives most of what is best*. It is quite different in Providence to what it is in Grace. Were everyone to get what they wished, the Arabian would have no sandy desert; the Laplander would not have to remain so long without the sun; there would not be so many toilsome days and wearisome nights endured. But however much you pray regarding God's providential dealings, the sun will continue, like a strong man, to run its race, and death will be the lot of the children of men. These outward things will roll on as they are. But let your earnest prayer be that the Sun of Righteousness (better far than that sun which is now shining upon you) may warm and enlighten your souls; that the wilderness and the solitary place may be glad and the desert rejoice and blossom as the rose, and that God will say to you, 'Be it unto thee even as thou wilt'.

But we may see that the Lord is more King-like still, when we consider that you would never receive these blessings unless He made you willing to do so. Do you ask wisdom? Well, He giveth liberally and upbraideth not. Are you murmuring and complaining? Are you saying, 'My leanness, my leanness!'? Well, look to it for you are not straitened in God but in yourselves. Only open your mouth wide and He will fill it. He will say to you, 'Be it unto thee even as thou wilt'.

Now these are three desires within the renewed soul. This woman's (of Canaan) daughter was grievously vexed with a devil. Jesus did not at the first grant her request – not to put a stumbling block in the way of her faith, but rather to bring it out more brightly. Now you are also grievously vexed with the devil and you require deliverance from him as the debtor does from the jailer, as the slave does from the tyrant, and as the traveller does from the robber that way-lays him. The renewed soul says, I would wish Jesus to be my Surety; I would wish Jesus to be my Lord, my Master, my King; and I would wish Jesus to be my companion to go with me all the way to Heaven.

Now, if you truly desire these things, you have been made willing. Once you were running away from God as Onesimus was from Philemon. Every step you took was further and further from your Father's house. Although you may be regular in the ordinances of religion, that is just as if Onesimus had looked over his shoulder, while all the time he was running away from his master's service. So you may be faithful in ordinances, but just mocking God, looking over your shoulder (as it were), and fleeing from Him. You need deliverance from the law. Justice, conscience and Satan cry – Pay me what thou owest. Now, who will save you? None but One. Even the highest angel could not be the surety of sinners, because every one of these blessed beings required to give all he can for himself, and could not pay the debts of another. So that none but Christ could be our Surety. And if you are willing that He should be yours, you will get the answer of my text, 'Be it unto thee even as thou wilt'.

It is a work of omnipotence to deliver you – God requires to put forth His almighty strength to save a soul. You perhaps think you are conferring an honour upon Jesus in allowing Him to subdue your sins and to sanctify you; but there is a great difference between nature and grace. Whenever you are renewed you become humbled. You see it is infinite condescension in the Lord to look upon the highest angel, far less to look upon such as you. Then run and throw yourself into His hands and you will receive the answer to my text, 'Be it unto thee even as thou wilt'.

Would you value not only your debts discharged and your lusts subdued, but heaven's society enjoyed? Would you wish Jesus to be your companion in the way? Then, 'Be it unto thee even as thou wilt'.

Nor would you live for ever in this outward house of clay. You would wish to be forever with the Lord.

What a miserable account I here give of a sermon which was so full and powerful. The Lord sanctify my memory and cause the savour of these rich words to remain with me.

Began to read last Saturday evening what I should have read long before now – Hetherington's *History of the Church of Scotland*. While reading, may my understanding be enlightened so that I may fully understand the great principles of which it treats, and may my heart be touched so that I may be more and more interested in the church of my fathers, and feel greatly for the afflictions of Joseph.

Wednesday evening, 28th February
Felt lately (which was perhaps owing to my being rather feeble for the past fortnight) that I might soon be called away. This used to be often and so much impressed upon my mind years ago. Although I have lived longer than I thought at that time I would, still I used to feel thankful for these presentiments. I thought it might be the Lord who put such into my mind to save me from my lethargy, and to remind me of the command, 'Whatsoever thy hand findeth to do, do it with all thy might'. O that having no continuing city here, I may be earnestly seeking one to come! Had a sweet letter on Monday from Eliza McCheyne in which she speaks of some scenes of the past. (Her affectionate kindness is often very affecting.) Heard also from Isabella Williamson regarding her marriage in the last week of March (which I was dreading) instead of the first week of April. She gave Tuesday the 25th as the day, which, however, is a mistake as Monday is the 25th. These two letters received at the same time completely upset me, so that my bursting heart could only find relief in a flood of tears.

Last Sabbath was a quiet day at home on account of the very heavy fall of snow. Two years that day it was since dear Johnnie departed 'to be with Christ, which is far better'. The events of that day were rising up before me, *among others the evening visit of one who was so faithful and yet so tender and sympathising in the home of sorrow*. Oh that Jesus would say to my troubled heart, 'Peace be still', and then there would be a great calm. May every pain be sanctified to me. Had a nice note also from Eliza Anne Ireland on Monday, in which she tells me that they have good hopes the Lord has been preparing her brother Alex to be with Himself. This I was rejoiced to hear. Truly our God is merciful and gracious. Had a note from Anne Clarke today asking Mamma and me to sew a square for a carpet, which it is proposed the Ladies of Scotland shall do for the Sustentation Fund. We shall be truly happy to aid in the work.

Saturday evening, 9th March

Mr Cook exchanged with Mr Bain last Sabbath. We had two plain gospel sermons from the latter – in the forenoon from the words, 'Deliver from going down into the pit; I have found a ransom'. In the afternoon he preached on the conversion of Lydia. The sufficiency and efficiency of the remedy God has provided in the Gospel of Jesus were clearly set forth. Attended the Presbytery at Couper on Thursday for the second time. Mr Ferguson gave a learned and interesting lecture on the first verse of the 8th chapter of Acts. He made allusion to Stephen and some things he said affected me not a little. *They seemed so applicable to one who was also filled with faith and the Holy Ghost, but who is now fallen asleep.*

We saw old Miss Whitson, who was very breathless, and to all appearances near her end. On coming away, when Mamma was speaking to her of the comforts of divine things, she acknowledged it all, and spoke as if it were the only source of comfort, but as if it were difficult to lay hold on them. She remarked that we should endeavour to say, 'Thy will be done', whether in light or in darkness. Oh, how diligently we should seek after assurance. For if our heart condemn us not then have we confidence toward God. Oh the misery of being deceived and the blessedness of having God's

Spirit witnessing with our spirit that we are the children of God. How often do I say with Newton,

> ''Tis a point I long to know,
> Oft it causes anxious thought,
> Do I love the Lord or no,
> Am I His or am I not?'

Saturday evening, 16th March

Last Sabbath forenoon, Mr Cook preached, I thought, a better sermon than most we had from him, on 'Godliness is profitable unto all things'. It is so in relieving the sorrows and afflictions of life; in sweetening creature comforts and giving pleasures peculiar to itself; in unnerving the sting of death; taking the victory from the grave, and also in preparing us for the world to come.

Mr MacDonald preached on Sabbath morning and preached in the afternoon from, 'We know that all things work together for good to them that love God'. A simple but animated sermon. He spoke to the Sabbath scholars on 'Confess your faults to one another...'. May I never forget a sentence which he quoted from an old book, 'Nearness to God is my felicity'. Oh that I may ever be able to say this also – to feel God to be my chief good, my exceeding joy, my portion, my all in all.

Mr MacDonald, Mr Gillies, Mr Bain, Mr Ferguson, Dr Cooper and Mr Cook dined here on Tuesday. Some of them were very lively. Oh to have a holy cheerfulness flowing from gladness of heart because of God's countenance being lifted on the soul!

At the meeting on Wednesday evening, on expounding at worship, Mr MacDonald made a few sweet remarks on, 'I beseech you as strangers and pilgrims, abstain from fleshly lusts...'. *He said that we were constantly trying to make this world our home and God was always trying not to make us do so.*

On the Tuesday forenoon, Mr Bain, Mr Gillies, Mr MacDonald and Mr Ferguson met here on business. Then they, with Dr Cooper and Mr Cook, dined with us afterwards. Mr Ferguson remained with us all night. May he prove a blessing to us and may we also be helpers to him. *It was a year that day according to the day of the week, since my valuable friend and kind counsellor took sick of his last illness*. It appears two or three years to me instead of one.

Monday evening, 18th March

When Mr Patrick Millar came in on Saturday night, could not help being at different times much affected because of his being associated with dear Robert McCheyne and having not seen Mr Millar since his death.

I felt I thought some enlargement in speaking to my class in the evening, and in asking the Lord to bless them anything I was enabled to say (however weakly spoken) which was according to His own mind and will. Oh to see once more the outward signs of concern among the scholars (which some speak against in revival) for then would I feel that the Lord was beginning to melt some hard hearts under the Word.

Saturday evening, 23rd March

Went to Dundee, where I have not been for a year past. I wanted to be present at dear Isabella Williamson's marriage on Wednesday evening. The sight of St Peter's spire, as we drove into town quite upset me. During the few days I was there, in the midst of everything else, the thought was constantly present before me *that he was away*. Walked in the afternoon to the dear spot where our friend's remains rest, and felt so overcome while standing there that I couldn't realise anything; but, oh, how applicable are his own words to himself:

> The precious dust beneath that lies,
> Shall at the Voice of Jesus rise,
> To meet the Bridegroom in the skies,
> There, there, we'll meet again.

With lingering steps and wistful looks I left the spot and even the outward walls of that dear church touched many a cord in my bosom and told many a tale to my aching heart.

Everything went on very happily at the marriage on Wednesday evening. I felt solemnised during the ceremony, and thought the presence of Jesus was there. In the afternoon Isabella and I were talking for a little of Christ's union to His people being so often illustrated by marriage. Ah! how close and endearing is this union and how enduring also. Oh that the Lord would make me to know assuredly that He has fulfilled that gracious word to me, 'I will betroth thee unto Me forever'. No man, angel or devil can draw away the soul that is united to Jesus, seeing this union is for ever.

Monday evening, 25th March 1844[2]

It is not easy to put down this date, for it is a year today by the day of the months (although last Saturday by the day of the week) since our beloved friend entered into rest. He no more feels a weak body, nor does he mourn over his own sins and over the sins of others. He has no longer sorrows to weigh down his tender spirit. He has been a year before the

2. The anniversary of Mr McCheyne's death

Throne, in the presence of that Jesus whom, not having seen, he loved. To him to live was Christ and to die was gain. But, Oh it seems to me like two or three years instead of one, since he left our earth. The Lord Himself make up to me what I have lost in him; for the more I see of others the more do I feel persuaded that I shall never see his like again. Oh that I had improved more under, and made greater use of all the grace given to him, but alas he is no longer here to say a faithful and searching, yet kind and tender word to me. O Lord, enable me from this day forward to go up from the wilderness leaning upon the Beloved, having my eye fixed intently on the Canaan beyond – that better and heavenly country.

Felt more enlargement, liberty and pleasure in teaching the girls than I usually do. They were very attentive and some of them interested, if not impressed and affected.

Thursday evening, 28th March
Truly I am a monument of God's mercy; for, considering my sloth and unpreparedness, He might have shut my mouth. Oh that His repeated goodness may lead me to repentance and that He would be pleased to show me some tokens for good among the scholars. I do long after their salvation. Lord, turn them and they shall be turned, draw them and they will run after Thee, for Jesus' sake, Amen.

We have had a sight a few weeks back of the second volume of R M McCheyne's 'Remains'. Felt the letters sweet and profitable. When looking into the book yesterday forenoon it opened at two different places, where he speaks plainly and faithfully of Achan's idols and besetting sins. Oh Lord, although Thy servant be dead, may he yet speak with power to my soul and grant that I may desire above all things not only that the guilt of all and every sin may be washed away, but that the power of them may be subdued also - every thought being brought into captivity to the obedience of Christ. Oh to be willing to part with everything for Him, although it be a right hand or a right eye.

May I deny myself and take up my cross and follow Him. The Lord enable me to say with Ephraim, 'What have I to do any more with idols?' Yea to lay aside every weight, and the sin that doth most easily beset me, and to run with patience the race that is set before me looking unto Jesus.

Papa brought out copies of the two volumes last evening and, being not very well today, have read all the 'Memoir'. Although I cannot but regret it is so much condensed, still, what is of it, is very precious and as I went along, felt it very quickening. *Oh to see sin, to prize the blood of sprinkling and pant after holiness as he did*. With Paul I would say, 'This one thing I do forgetting the things that are behind...'. Oh Lord, lead me in the footsteps of the flock. Make me to be a follower of them who through faith and patience are now inheriting the promises.

Read within the last few days a short but affecting account of the experiences of George Philips. In some parts though it resembled my own, and that I might say with him, 'God willing, Christ willing, the Spirit willing, I willing, and *yet my desires not satisfied*'. But still, I cannot be willing to part with everything for Christ; there must be a besetting sin trying to get the mastery over me. Lord make me willing in the day of Thy power, and although I am as weak as water in myself, yet perfect Thy strength in my weakness; and cause me ever to remember that word, 'Whosoever he be of you that forsaketh not all that he hath, cannot be my disciple'.

Monday, 8th April

Mr John Bain recently preached an excellent and solemn sermon on, 'If the righteous scarcely be saved where shall the ungodly and the sinner appear?' In the afternoon he preached a sweet and comforting sermon from the words, 'Come unto me, all ye that labour and are heavy laden and I will give you rest'. Enjoyed much all he said. I felt there was a weight in his words; for he seemed softened by affliction. Oh Lord, forbid that I should at any time be insensible, but grant that I may ever lie low under the stroke of Thy hand.

Did not enjoy being with my class in the evening. Taught with great discomfort to myself and I am persuaded with little profit to others. My heart was unmelted and mouth closed. How true it is that, 'Out of the abundance of the heart the mouth speaketh', and no wonder that I often speak with such coldness when my heart is so little affected with divine things. Oh Lord Jesus, give me a heart overflowing with love to Thee, then shall I be full of good matter; then I will be weary of forbearing and not able to stay. Holy Father, open Thou my lips, and my mouth shall show forth Thy praise.

Monday evening, 29th April

On the evening of yesterday fortnight, listened with pleasure to Mr Caird teaching my class, on the first Adam who was of the 'earth, earthy', being a type of the second Adam 'the Lord from Heaven'. He enlarged on his offices as prophet, priest and king. Mr Caird said afterwards that he thought the reason why Adam was created on the sixth day and not before, was that he might enjoy a whole day's communion with God and that he might begin his life in the spiritual service of God.

Mr Caird addressed, shortly, the whole school, on David

showing kindness to Mephibosheth. He took the story as illustrative of God's kindness to sinners. Jonathan's son was helpless and required to be brought to the house. David showed him kindness for the sake of another. He was to eat bread at the table of the king continually. This resembles God's kindness to us for the sake of His beloved Son. How unspeakably blessed are these words, 'sitting in heavenly places in Christ, that in the ages to come He might show the exceeding riches of His grace, in His kindness toward us through Christ Jesus'.

Went to Dundee on the Wednesday to spend a week with Isabella, and to attend the communion which I had not done for eighteen months. Heard Mr Manson preach an excellent sermon on the forenoon of the Fast day from these words, 'My God, My God, why hast Thou forsaken Me?' His divisions were: The nature of this desertion; the causes of this desertion; and the effects that flow from this desertion. He made several allusions both in prayer and discourse to the dear departed and to happy days gone by. As for myself it was so overcoming to be in St Peter's again. I felt very much agitated and confused, but more calm and composed in the afternoon. Mr Bonar's exposition of Psalm 102 was precious, and his sermon on Philippians 2, verses 1 and 2, 'If there be therefore any consolation in Christ', was rich and full. He spoke of resting on the mercies of the Godhead as on a pillow.

Heard Mr A Ferguson in the evening at Dudhope. He preached a striking and interesting sermon from Matthew 2, verses 1 and 2, 'Now when Jesus was born...'. He spoke of Jesus being born the hope of glory in our hearts which by nature are as vile as the stable at Bethlehem. He mentioned how God's mercies are always seasonable. Christ was born in the day of Herod the king when the cause of God was at a low ebb. He ended on the sweet thought that when we entered the gates of the heavenly Jerusalem our joyous cry would somewhat resemble that of the wise men, 'Where is Jesus that we may worship Him?' Oh Lord, hasten the happy day when all the kingdoms of the earth shall bow down before this blessed Prince of peace; yet when every nation shall serve Him.

On the Friday evening Mr Bonar took for his subject the parable of the ten virgins. He spoke chiefly on our being ready for the Table.

On Saturday heard Mr Samuel Millar in St David's. A very suitable sermon for a preparation Saturday on, 'O my Father, if it be possible, let this cup pass from Me'. Spoke of Christ's greater sufferings beginning then, for it says, 'He began to be sorrowful'. The load that was lying upon Him was so infinite that His blessed body gave way under it; and although He had been looking at it in types and prophecies for hundreds of years, yet we find that 'He was sore dismayed' when He came under it.

He reminded believers that through much tribulation they would enter the kingdom of heaven. They would have cups of sorrow put into their hands, but then how different from the cup Jesus had to drink, for while there was a curse in His there would be no curse in theirs. How affecting thus to meditate on the awful sufferings of the Son of God. Oh to understand better the love which led God to give up Jesus, and which led Jesus to give up Himself to such agony; yea to comprehend with all saints what is its breadth, length, depth and height.

Mr Islay Burns preached on Sabbath a tender sermon on, 'And I, if I be lifted up from the earth, will draw all men unto

Me'. The first Table service was on, 'Arise my love, my fair one, and come away'. Had not much peace when I sat down at the Table, but was comforted by these passages coming to mind, 'I have blotted out, as a thick cloud, thy transgressions and as a cloud thy sin; return unto Me for I have redeemed thee'. Mr Bain also gave an animated Table service from, 'Seeing then we are compassed about with so great a cloud of witnesses'. He alluded to one who ran the race in a way that few did, and who would yet be a witness for or against us. Mr Burns gave a short address at the end from, 'Arise, let us go hence', hence to active duty; hence to glory at last. It was altogether a sweet day; and although often overcome, it was not like bygone communions. The people seemed still and solemnised and in a tender frame. Notwithstanding the sad change in St Peter's I still felt the place blessed, and different from any other church I had been to. It was good to be there.

But O I have a wicked heart and a tempting devil, for after coming from the Table my thoughts were wandering much, and my heart going after idols. Oh Lord, pardon the great iniquity of my holy things. Enable me ever to watch and pray that I enter not into temptation.

Mr Gillies preached a good sermon on Monday from, 'Why are ye troubled?'. He spoke of the interest that believers have in Christ. He is their Bridegroom, Friend, sympathising High Priest, and mystical Head. He then told them to consider what Jesus had already done *in giving Himself for them and giving Himself to them.* They must think also of what He had promised to do, what He is now doing, and what He is preparing for them above. When the Lord's people, he said, give way to troubles, it dishonours Christ and grieves Him. What a display, he said, of the love and tenderness and desire for the happiness of His people Jesus has given in this wise. When you are troubled, not only muse on these topics, but pray for the Comforter. 'I would,' said the preacher, 'say to the unbelievers that the Lord Jesus just reverses the order of the text to you. He would say to them, "Why are ye not troubled?" You have everything to trouble you. How often in days gone by did the Lord make the last day the great day of the feast?' The Monday evening meeting was solemn indeed; causing us to say, 'Thou hast kept the good wine till now'. Shall I ever know such sweet days again on earth?

Friday, 28th June
Was privileged again a week past last Sabbath to partake of the Lord's Supper at Rattray. Heard a precious sermon from Mr Gillies on Song 1, verse 12. The principal divisions were: The titles given to Christ; the sweet fellowship that the Bride has with her Kindly Spouse; the holy and blessed effects which fellowship with Christ had upon her own soul. Oh to be so taught as to discern with a spiritual eye, the meaning of that rich book – the Song of Solomon. There were sweet Table services on, 'All things are ready', and 'Ye do show forth the Lord's death till He come'. Mr Gillies gave an address also on that remarkable suitable passage, Exodus 23, verses 20 and 21, 'Behold I send an angel before thee', but being so much worn out, I could not enjoy it as I wished. Mr Ferguson preached in the evening on the three last verses of Genesis, chapter 8. He said with regard to this offering that it was an appointed, an atoning, a substitutionary and a typical offering.

Although I did not feel so much exercised as on the last communion Sabbath spent there, still it was a sweet day, and were it not for my wandering heart it might have been sweeter still. On the Monday Mr Bain preached a very good sermon from Hebrews chapter 7, verse 25. He dwelt on the extent of God's salvation; the objects of it; the greatest sinner may be saved by it. He saves from all the consequences of sin; He saves in spite of all opposition; He saves to the end. He dwelt also in the security of the believer since this salvation rests on Christ's life and intercession.

Wednesday, 3rd July

On the Thursday following the communion at Rattray, we had a meeting of the Sabbath school in the open air. It began with praise and prayer. After remaining above an hour on the green, we adjourned to the church, where Mr Ferguson first addressed us on the subject of prayer. He told the children of the kite that the philosopher sent up into the sky as illustrative of the power of prayer. He bade them send up prayers to God who was seated upon a throne which was to them a mercy seat. Then He would enrich them with durable riches. 'Pray,' he said, 'to be forgiven, pray to be brought near to Christ, pray to live a useful life, pray to have a happy death. How are we to pray? With reverence, with boldness, with humility, with faith, with earnestness, with perseverance. All, however far in sin, should pray "Behold the Lord's hand is not shortened that it cannot save." Manasseh had gone far down in sin, but the Lord's arm took hold of him. "Neither is His ear heavy that it cannot hear." Jonah prayed in the whale's belly. His prayer came through the fish and through the sea, and through the air and through the clouds, and reached the ear of God.'

Mr Gillies then spoke of King Josiah, and reminded the children that although they could not be kings in this world they might be kings in glory. Josiah was early pious. Mr Gillies sweetly compared those who were early in Christ to rose buds, the sweetest flower in the garden. Jesus loved those peculiarly who came to Him in the morning of their days. This young king loved the Word of God. He also died a safe and happy death for we are told that he came to his grave in peace.

Mr Bain also addressed them shortly on the Bible being God's letter to us; that it teaches us two things which he illustrated by the beautiful story of the minister in the North[3] who told a young girl to pray in these words, 'Lord, show me myself', and 'Lord, show me Thyself'. Mr MacDonald concluded by speaking on the two ways. 'It is easier,' he said, 'to enter on the one way than the other; the one gate is wide, the other is strait. On the latter gate are words of prohibition written such as, "Except a man be born again he cannot enter the Kingdom of God". It is easier to proceed on the one way than the other; the one is broad, the other narrow; the one is downhill, the other is uphill. The one is more crowded than the other. The one is the way of sinful pleasure; the other of happiness and peace. The one leads to hell, the other to Heaven.' May the fruit of this meeting be unto holiness and the end thereof everlasting life.

14th July

On the Saturday Mr Ferguson preached a very refreshing sermon on, 'Ye are the temple of the living God'. He spoke on the nature of this temple; the owner of this temple; and the tenant of this temple. Only had time to speak on the first head but it was very grand – some noble thoughts in it. Regarding the nature of the temple he said that it was spiritual, purchased, prepared. What he said concerning the service of

3. Mr Hector MacPhail, Resolis.

the Spirit being secured by Christ was very sweet.

On the Sabbath Mr MacDonald preached an animated sermon from II Samuel, chapter 18, verse 3, 'Thou art worth ten thousand of us'. 'Jesus,' he said, 'is worth ten thousand of us in the purity of His character; in the depth of His wisdom; in the intensity of His love; in the greatness of His power; in the largeness of His gifts and in the brightness of His glory. If He is worth ten thousand of us surely He is worth being remembered by us. He should be preferred to all else besides. How awful is the guilt of rejecting such a precious gift as Christ is.'

Did not feel much happiness before going to the Table; but when seated there and asking the Lord to manifest His Love to me, I was greatly comforted by these words sweetly coming to me with power as from the Good Shepherd, 'I have loved thee with an everlasting Love, therefore with loving kindness have I drawn thee.' And also these, 'I will guide thee with My counsel, and afterwards receive thee into glory'. Oh that both of these precious promises may be indeed mine. Oh that I may have been chosen in Christ before the foundation of the world, and be among those whom He loves to the end.

In the evening Mr Millar, Clunie, preached a long and excellent sermon from the 29th verse of the 22nd chapter of Matthew, 'Jesus answered and said unto them, ye do err not knowing the scriptures nor the power of God'. He exhorted us to be students of the Word of God and to read it as if we were the only persons in the world that did read it. I resolved that I would read the scriptures more. Oh to feel more and more every day the power of its precious truths, and see the mind of the Spirit within. It is not enough to say, 'How love I Thy law', but also to add, 'It is my meditation all the day'.

On the Monday Mr Baxter preached an excellent sermon on 1st John, chapter 3, verse 2, 'Beloved now are we the sons of God, and it doth not yet appear what we shall be'. 'Believers,' he said, 'are the sons of God by regeneration in virtue of their union with Christ, and by adoption. As for their present dignity and privileges they have a son's interest in God; they have the spirit of adoption; they are taught of God; they are fed by Jehovah. He also chastens them. All of them have a title to the inheritance above. Though their prospects are so wonderful they do not know much about heaven. We must be there before we can tell what it is, but there are many things certain about it. Christ is there. The Bible tells believers this and so does Christian experience. They know it is a place where His glory is to be seen. It is also a place where they shall be perfectly like Christ and there shall be no Canaanite then in the house of the Lord.'

Oh to have clearer evidence that I am among the children, and that I am being prepared for the time when Jesus shall appear, and when all the family shall be like Him, when they shall see Him as He is.

Friday, 16th August

Yesterday fortnight we returned from a little northern tour, on which we set out on Tuesday morning. Our party consisted of our own family, Mr A C Dunn (who had been with us for two or three weeks), Mr and Mrs Moncur, with Sarah Williamson and Mr Lamb. The weather was rather wet, which, of course, lessened our pleasure. Still we enjoyed it much. The first day we had a beautiful drive to Kenmore, and when on our way visited the Falls of Moness, which are very pretty. The forenoon of Wednesday we spent in wandering over the lovely grounds of Taymouth. It was a sweet calm day.

It was also my birthday, which to me is always a solemn day. Oh for a tender heart to mourn over the sins of past years, and also for a thankful spirit to praise the Lord for all the way by which He has led me. Surely I should raise up a stone of remembrance – an Ebenezer – for hitherto hath the Lord helped me. And as I advance in years, may I grow in grace and in the knowledge of my Lord and Saviour Jesus Christ. If spared to see another year may I be very different from what I am just now, much further on the way to Zion, with earthly things more below my feet and heavenly things more in my eye, running with a quicker step the race that is set before me 'looking unto Jesus'. Oh Lord, fashion me according to Thine own blessed mind and will, and enable me whatsoever I do in word and deed, to do all to Thy praise and glory. Oh Lord give me a real heart-felt desire to serve Thee in this world. Enable me to do so in whatever situation I am; and if it be thy will, O Lord Jesus, open up a way speedily wherein I may be employed much in Thy sweet service. I would live to the praise of Thy glorious grace, desiring above all things Thy name may be magnified.

On the afternoon of this same day – Wednesday – had a lovely drive on the banks of the Tummel and Garry. Next day, on our way from Dalnacardoch to Blair Atholl, we visited the Falls of Bruar, which are wilder and grander than those of Moness, though not so sweet nor the crags so richly wooded. The finest part of the road was the Pass of Killiecrankie between Blair Atholl and Dunkeld. The hills are so high and yet so richly and beautifully clothed. We were all very tired however when we reached home late on Thursday night, yet delighted with all the lovely scenery. What a beautiful earth this is were it not stained with sin! What a powerful Saviour must He be whose hand formed it!

'All things made by Him, and without Him not anything made that was made.' How sweet to be able to say in looking upon the wonders of nature, my Redeemer gave them all their loveliness, yea, my Father made them all.

Saturday, 28th September

Mr Main left us on Tuesday after being with us from the Wednesday before. Enjoyed his visit exceedingly, indeed almost more than I have done any other since our late beloved friend was with us. His ministrations in the sanctuary were very edifying; his expositions of scripture in the family also edifying. Oh that his visit may have been greatly blessed both to us and to the people, and the Lord give him as he himself prayed – to see in Eternity some fruits of his short ministrations here.

He commented in a very sweet manner on the first chapter of Philippians and preached a lively and elevating sermon on, 'To him that overcometh I will give to eat of the tree of life which is in the midst of the Paradise of God'. He preached a searching and practical sermon in the afternoon on, 'What shall I do to be saved?' He delivered a very powerful sermon from the verse, 'Which hope we have as an anchor of the soul both sure and steadfast'. His introduction was on the nature of the grace of hope. He spoke of it as being the solace and sweetener of life. He spoke of the voyage of life, and that everything depends on the character of the ground in which the anchor is cast.

The anchor which is the believer's hope enters into that which is within the veil. It is fastened on Christ, and rests on His finished work; but if everything depends on the character of the ground in which the anchor is cast, and if Christ is a rock, how then can we cast an anchor in Him? *Ah, but the rock is cleft. He is the rock of ages cleft for this very purpose that a poor sinner may place his hope in him.* All God's wrath has been already spent on Christ. The world are anchoring the eternal on the temporal and shifting; but our anchor must be cast on immortality and on the abiding.

His hope keeps the believer steadfast. A ship needs an anchor at the harbour if she is to trade at the port. So the believer needs an anchor when he comes into contact with the world. The way to overcome the world is to have his hope within the veil. Let his eye be fixed on the glories above, and he will be kept steadfast. Let him have the tree of life in his view, and the flowers of earth will appear to have little beauty. Let him drink of the cup of salvation, and the cup of this world's pleasures will seem little to him. The world says religion is a dull thing but the believer does not think so when he can almost grasp his palm of victory. The vessel needs an anchor in the midst of a storm, so does the believer in the midst of affliction. Do sickness, bereavement, calamity, death come? Then you feel the benefit of your anchor, your hope, within the veil. There is a solemn verse by which to try ourselves as to the character of our hope, 'If thou hast run with the footmen and they have wearied thee...'.

We can imagine no greater punishment than that a man be left to toss ten years on the sea without a compass or without a rudder, and with neither sun nor stars appearing; but what would that be compared to be cast out of the sea on the fiery waves of the burning lake, in the blackness of darkness for ever? If we will not come to Jesus who is the only Saviour of the soul, we are leaving Calvary, and for that reason we shall have to shed bitter tears through all eternity.

We parted with Mr Main with very much regret, and with the earnest desire that he may be greatly beloved of the Lord, his own soul richly watered, and his dear people given showers of blessing.

Saturday evening, 2nd November

Was taken ill last Thursday, and confined to bed for a few days; but the attack was much milder than those of the past years. I am almost well again. The Lord deals very gently. Oh that my hard heart might be softened by this short season of sickness. Received a kind letter from dear Eliza McCheyne yesterday, giving a delightful account of their communion week. The Lord be praised for thus gladdening her spirit. May our approaching communion season be of a similar nature. O Holy Spirit make it a season of great quickening to me, a resurrection time to my poor dead lifeless soul. Finished reading Mr Breay's 'Memoir'. He was a minister of the Church of England in Birmingham. Enjoyed many of his letters especially. A very spiritually minded man.

Read also Mrs Wallace Duncan's 'Memoir' the second time. Enjoyed it more than the first reading of it, and trust I felt quickened by it, and desirous of copying all in her that was worthy of imitation. Oh to follow those who through faith and patience are now inheriting the promises.

Friday, 29th November

A week past last Lord's day was the Sacramental Sabbath here. I tried to renew my covenant with the Lord at His Table and to give myself and all that I am and have to His service. But, alas, how coldly done. Nevertheless, O Lord, for Thine own name's sake, and because of Thy rich mercy in Christ, accept of me and make me altogether Thine, and if it be Thy Holy will, cause me to be useful in my day and generation.

Heard Dr Candlish on Thursday afternoon from Psalm

32, verses 1 and 2, 'Blessed is he whose transgression is forgiven, whose sin is covered. Blessed is the man unto whom the Lord imputeth not iniquity and in whose spirit there is no guile'. A clear, full gospel sermon. Each one of those expressions, 'transgression', 'sin', 'iniquity', and 'guile' rises in meaning above the others – the mercy, holiness and justice of God are all seen in them. The preacher spoke of the spiritual character or frame of mind connected with this state – 'in whose spirit there is no guile'.

What kind of guile is that which the natural man has? It is expressed in these words, 'if we say that we have fellowship with Him, and walk in darkness, we lie and do not tell the truth. If we say that we have no sin, we deceive ourselves and the truth is not in us' (1 John 1:6-8). There are two kinds of guile that hinder men from believing – chapter 2, verse 4, 'He that saith I know Him, and keepeth not His commandments, is a liar and the truth is not in him'. There is a kind of guile to which professing Christians are liable.

What are the elements or ingredients of the blessedness here spoken of. Verses 3 and 5, 'When I kept silent my bones waxed old, through my roaring all the day long. I acknowledged my sin unto Thee, and mine iniquity have I not hid. I said, I will confess my transgressions unto the Lord; and Thou forgavest the iniquity of my sin'. This purpose of confession ended the strife. David was done forever with trying to patch a righteousness of his own.

Another aspect of this blessedness is security in trouble. 'Thou art my hiding place; Thou shalt preserve me from trouble; Thou shalt compass me about with songs of deliverance'. Believers are the Lord's hidden ones. Just as when a child is in any danger, without a moment's thought as if by instinct, it runs at once and hides in its mother's bosom; so when the child of God is in trouble his first impulse is to hide in God, Who is our refuge and a very present help in trouble.

Another aspect of this blessedness is found in the Lord's guidance (verse 8), 'I will instruct thee and teach thee with mine eye'. When you have sinned, does Christ's eye make you weep as it did Peter? Or when you are hesitating as to what path you should take, does Christ's eye when it meets you make you start back? And when you are unwilling to make some sacrifice for Jesus' sake, when His eye looks upon you, does it stir you up, as if He were saying to you, 'Will you grudge to sacrifice for me who died for thee?' But if you are asking the world's question, 'May I?' and 'Must I?' then you are renouncing the privilege of children. You should rather stand fast in the liberty wherewith Christ hath made us free, for God hath not given us the spirit of fear; but of power, and of love and of a sound mind.

Dr Candlish gave us a most delightful sermon again in the evening from John 7, verses 37-39, 'In the last day that great day of the feast, Jesus stood and cried saying, "If any man thirst let him come unto Me and drink."' He began by speaking of the feast of tabernacles, in allusion to which these words of Isaiah are written, 'Therefore with joy shall ye draw water out of the wells of salvation'. And in the last day of the feast, One is seen standing in the midst and crying, 'If any man thirst...'. The language of the people was, 'who will show us any good?'. And Jesus told them that if they would drink of the water which He would give them, it would be within them a well of water springing up unto everlasting life. 'He that believeth on Me as the scripture hath said, out of his belly shall flow rivers of living waters. But this spake He of the Spirit, which they that believe on Him should receive; for the Holy Ghost was not yet given; because that Jesus was not yet glorified.' Enquire in what sense the Holy Ghost is here said to be given and received.

First, in respect of His personal presence. He is a living person, Romans 15, verse 30, 'Now I beseech you brethren, for the Lord Jesus Christ's sake and for the love of the Spirit'.

Second, in respect of His powerful working. He works upon all the faculties, the understanding, conscience, heart and will.

Third, in respect of His blessed fruit. The fruit of the Spirit is love, joy, peace, longsuffering, etc. The fruit of the Spirit working on the soul consists of our being convinced of our sin; of our minds being enlightened in the knowledge of Christ; and the issue of the process in that we are persuaded and enabled to embrace Jesus Christ freely offered to us in the gospel. There is here the simplicity of a little child.

Let us enquire also what is the connection here between the Holy Spirit being given, and Christ being glorified. 'For the Holy Ghost was not yet given, because that Jesus was not yet glorified.' He was given in the Old Testament times, on the faith of Christ being glorified. Abraham saw Jesus' day afar off and was glad. The Holy Ghost is given because He is Christ's purchase; satisfaction being given by Jesus, He purchased the Spirit for His people. He is Christ's special gift. In regard to the outpouring on the day of Pentecost, it is written of Jesus, 'Therefore being by the right hand of God exalted, and having received of the Father the promise of the Holy Ghost, He hath shed forth this, which ye now see and hear'.

But specially is the Holy Ghost given because He is Christ's witness. 'He shall glorify Me, for He shall receive of Mine and shall show it unto you.' 'But when the Comforter is come whom I will send...' He testifies of Jesus as a complete Saviour, that He is able to save to the uttermost all that come unto God by Him. He testifies of His birth, His baptism, His life, His sufferings, His death, His burial, His resurrection, His ascension, in short, to show us that all we need is treasured up in Him.

What is the connection between the Holy Ghost being received, and the exercise of faith? 'This spake He of the Spirit which they that believe on Him should receive.' There is a certain measure of the Holy Ghost even without faith, for unless the Spirit draw us we would never lay hold on Jesus; so that the Lord gives the Holy Ghost even to those who are not believers. But in this God is sovereign. He says, 'My Spirit will not always strive with man.'

I beseech you, said Dr Candlish, not to presume on the dispensation of the Spirit. But, children of God, if you are asked what is the connection between the Holy Ghost being given and your believing in Jesus? You may answer, faith unites me to Jesus and being one with Him I receive the Spirit. Another reason is my faith interests me in the ever-lasting covenant. All the promises of God are to be Yea and Amen in Christ Jesus. One of the promises, for example, is, 'I will pour water on him that is thirsty and floods upon the dry ground'. The wicked is an illustration of what we have been saying, regarding the difference in the way in which the Holy Ghost is given to believers and unbelievers. The world receive the bounties of God's providence as well as His children, for it is written, 'He maketh His sun to shine on the evil and on the good and sendeth rain on the just and on the unjust'. And so the unconverted sometimes receive common influences of God's Spirit, whereas the believer receives the Holy Ghost on the footing of a covenant engagement. 'We are sealed with the Holy Spirit of promise' and

He will continue it to you for His own name's sake.

Notice the measure and manner of this indwelling. 'He that believeth on me as the scriptures have said, out of his belly shall flow rivers of living water.' There are two particulars here regarding believers. First, they have the source of their joy within themselves. They do not need to draw from those broken cisterns, that can hold no water. They have the fountains of life itself to which to repair. It is 'Christ within you the hope of glory'. It was a great blessing to the Israelites to have a flowing stream following them all the way through the wilderness, which Rock, we are told, was Christ. It is your privilege to have the well within you. But if Jesus be within you, consider what should the streams be that flow from this fountain; not shallow but broad streams; not stagnant but living water. These waters are your Christian comforts – peace, joy, hope. They are your Christian graces – faith, love, obedience, delighting in God's law, meekness with long-suffering. If you are languishing, come to Christ again to be revived and if these waters are flowing copiously in your heart then blessed are ye. And what great blessings you may be to the dry ground around you! When the Holy Ghost came down in such abundance on the early church, we are told what the effect was, 'Fear came on every soul and many wonders and signs were done by the Apostles'. This sermon I enjoyed more than I can express. It was a rich feast to me indeed.

Mr Arnot, Glasgow, afterwards addressed us from the words, 'Christ loved the church and gave Himself for it; that He might sanctify and cleanse it with the washing of water by the word, that He might present it to himself a glorious church'. This, he said, will be a great presentation day. When any are presented to an earthly sovereign, they usually require to be high born, and so those who will be presented on that day, are sons and daughters of the King of kings. Again, those who are presented to an earthly sovereign are generally rich, and so those who will be presented on that day have the unsearchable riches of Christ. Again, those who are presented to an earthly sovereign usually require to have a court dress, and someone already at court to introduce them. Those who will be presented on that day are clothed in the righteousness of God and will be presented by Christ Himself. Those who are to be presented on that day are to be, 'without spot or wrinkle or any such thing'. Then you should seek to be holy now, recline on the bosom of Jesus, for no sin can be there. Ye are left a little while in the world to do the Lord's work. Ye are the salt of the earth. Ye are His reflectors. He says, 'I am glorified in them.' The dying Jacob refused to follow the desire of Joseph in placing his hands on the children. He said, 'I know it, my son, I know it.' And so perhaps some of you who are God's children may feel that He is crossing you in your desires, and you may be saying to Him, 'Not so my Father'; but you should feel satisfied with all His dealings, for He knoweth what is best for you; and will say to you, 'I know it, my son, I know it'.

On the Sabbath evening Mr Arnot preached an interesting sermon from John 19, verse 18, 'Where they crucified Him and two others with Him; on either side one and Jesus in the midst'. Look, he said, at Jesus in the midst, when covenanting with the Father in the eternal council. Again in the garden of Eden, He was in the midst when God gave Him in the promise that the seed of the woman should bruise the head of the serpent. Again we see Jesus in the midst at the times of the Old Testament saints, when we are told that Abraham saw His day afar off and was glad; when He appeared to Moses in the burning bush; to Joshua as the Captain of the Lord of Hosts; to Jacob as the angel of the covenant. He was in the midst in the fiery furnace with the holy children when there was One seen like unto the Son of God. And then in the fulness of the times, when He was twelve years old, He was in the midst of the Doctors in the temple who were both hearing Him and asking Him questions. On the Cross He was in the midst and now He is in the midst of the Throne.

Tuesday, 25th March 1845
It is two years since our invaluable friend entered into rest. It was an event which must ever be a solemn and affecting one to me. The Lord took to Heaven one who had been blessed more to me than all else in the world besides. Thanks be unto Thy name, O Lord, for all Thou didst for him and by him, and for all that my poor soul received from Thee through him. And may my remembrance of him, although often sorrowful and sometimes as if to crush my spirit, ever humble and quicken me, and urge me on in the way of life.

Today finished reading his 'Memoir' for the third time. O Lord, grant that this record of Thy faithful servant's journey through this vale of tears may be greatly and universally blessed of Thee, especially to those who are engaged in the glorious work of the ministry; that by it they may be led to cultivate greater holiness of walk and conversation, and to long more for the glory of Jesus in the salvation of souls.

Sabbath, 6th April
A beautiful spring day. Oh that the Sun of righteousness would shine as brightly upon my soul as that sun now does upon this world of ours. Although it is so lovely, I am not permitted to visit the House of prayer. Indeed, I have only

been once within the courts of the Lord's House since the middle of January owing to a tedious illness. Was better a fortnight ago and was out at church; but have relapsed since and am still very weak. Although my illness has not been very severe, yet it has been long continued. Great exhaustion accompanies the cough. Forbid, O my Father, that this season should pass over without being greatly blessed to me. How I regret that the quiet hours have not been more improved; but I often felt so stupid and languid that I could scarcely fix my mind on divine things. Yet blessed be the name of the Lord when at any time very ill, and inclined to be disquieted, He seemed to be gently whispering peace, so that I was thus comforted of God. But, Oh, I would earnestly desire that I might grow much at this time, especially in the knowledge of Jesus, Whom to know is life eternal. Alas! I am slow indeed to learn. If I have been taught anything at this time, it is more of my own guilt and corruption. I am nothing and can do nothing. I am completely without strength, but it was for such that Jesus died. And Oh that this knowledge of my weakness may lead me to embrace with simpler joy than ever a full Saviour, and to say with an understanding heart, 'In the Lord have I righteousness and strength'. But Oh Most Gracious God, suffer me not I beseech Thee to deceive myself. May I be truly one with Jesus. May I be dwelling in Christ and may Christ be formed in me the hope of glory. Most wonderful union! Oh Lord if I am Thine through Thy dear Son, may my life and walk and conversation be as it becometh the gospel. May every thought, word and action be conformed to its blessed rules. Blessed Spirit breathe into my soul the breath of life, and cause me to live anew, departing from all iniquity, and following after all that is pure and lovely and of good report.

Sabbath evening, 4th May

It is now nearly four months since this illness made its appearance. Oh Lord grant that I may never be impatient under Thy dealings, and enable me to ask in a humble enquiring spirit – not in a murmuring one – 'Wherefore contendest Thou with me?' If I have a strong desire to live a life of usefulness in the world, then Oh Lord Thou must have implanted that desire; and yet it seems to me as if Thou wert leading me by a way that I know not. If Thou are really leading me, then all is well.

> Guide me, O Thou great Jehovah,
> Pilgrim through this barren land.

And Oh grant me the sanctified use of all Thy dealings and may my will be lost in God's.

> Sweet to be passive in His hands,
> And know no will but His.

Oh Lord, prepare my understanding and heart, by giving me much knowledge and great devotedness so that I may spend my days in Thy service on earth, if this be Thy will, or if Thou art soon to call me Home, may my soul be made meet for the inheritance of the saints in light.

I heard Dr Candlish, when in Dundee a fortnight past, preach a truly delightful sermon on the 'Heavenly places'. It was most interesting, and I enjoyed it exceedingly. Finished reading last Sabbath the 'Life of Joseph Alleine', who seemed indeed to have his conversation in heaven. He appeared to pass his life in adoring contemplations of God's love; and yet he was most devoted and active in the service of his Lord. In the latter part especially of his short life – I think he only lived to the age of thirty-four – he almost seemed as if he were already an inhabitant of the New Jerusalem, and joined in the praises of the Redeemer before the Throne.

Heard an excellent sermon from Mr Gillies last Sabbath on these words, 'And the children of Israel did eat manna forty years in the wilderness, yea, they did eat manna until they came into the borders of the land of Canaan', viewing the manna as a type of Christ – very precious. Lord, evermore give me this bread. On the afternoon of today he preached an excellent sermon from the words, 'Ye are not your own, ye are bought with a price'. It was very practical and quickening. Oh Lord, impress the words of the text in my heart, and may they never be forgotten by me night or day.

Bridge of Allan – Sabbath, 22nd June

Last Sabbath the Lord's Supper was dispensed in Rattray and we attended there. Felt very doubtful as to whether I should partake of the ordinances, feeling that I was utterly devoid of a right frame of mind and had almost resolved not to do so; but as the day advanced I felt more comfort in thinking of going to the Table. However, owing to the heat and the great crowd, as well as the oppression in my chest, Mamma thought it better not to remain. We returned at the end of the First Table service. Perhaps the Lord ordered it thus as a punishment for my sloth – or in mercy – that I might not profane His Holy Table.

Mr Gillies preached an excellent sermon from, 'Truth Lord, yet the dogs eat of the crumbs that fall from the master's table'. Lord Jesus ever feed my soul out of Thine own hand. Mr Gillies fenced the Tables from John II, verses 55-56, showing that one duty before coming to the feast was to purify ourselves; and one duty when we had come was to seek that Jesus might be present there. He also spoke a word of comfort to timid souls from the 51st Psalm, 'The sacrifices of God are a broken spirit; a broken and a contrite heart, O God, Thou wilt not despise', telling them that a broken spirit suited a broken saviour. The subjects of his Table service were, 'Ye are come to the blood of sprinkling which speaketh better things than that of Abel'. And, 'They shall go from strength to strength, every one of them in Zion appeareth before God'. This latter part I felt, to be peculiarly sweet and comforting.

In the evening, Mr Ferguson of Alyth, preached a most delightful sermon from these blessed words, 'The Lamb is the Light thereof'. Some of his thoughts were very rich. O blessed Lamb of God, be Thou the light of my heart in this dark world, and through grace, prepare me for dwelling in that land of which Thou art now, and will be, the light through everlasting ages.

Sabbath evening, 27th July

Went to town last Wednesday, to see dear Isabella and her baby. Was in St Peter's on Thursday evening. A very, very thin audience. How changed in regard to the numbers that used to attend the Thursday meetings. *I felt it solemnising to be here, and as if it were indeed a sanctuary where the goings of our God had been often seen.* This day dear Isabella's infant was to be given to the Lord in baptism. May He accept the gift and make her His own for ever.

Wednesday, 31st July

This day, twenty-four years ago, I was born into a world of sin and sorrow. How long have I lived and to how little purpose! With how many mercies, temporal and spiritual, has the Lord crowned me, and yet how unfaithful have I been and how continually have I departed from Him. Oh that every sin of my past life may be washed away in His own blood. Lord, prepare me for whatever is before me this year, and grant that the life I may henceforth live in the flesh may be by the faith of the Son of God who - I trust I can say - loved me and gave Himself for me.

Monday evening, 8th September

It is four weeks today since A C Dunn, accompanied by his sister and Mr Fraser, left us for Dunkeld. O that every painful feeling I experienced at parting with dear friends may be sanctified in drawing me closer to the ever compassionate Jesus; who is the same yesterday, today, and forever. May He prepare me for that blessed Land from which the redeemed shall never depart; that glorious city where they shall be made pillars in the temple of their God, and out of which they shall never go.

I left the pleasant city of Edinburgh – where, with Mamma I spent a month – with much regret. Not a little sorry to say farewell to dear friends. But with none did I feel so much to part as with dear Eliza McCheyne, for my affections are entwined around her in no ordinary degree. Will it ever be ordered that our lots be cast near each other? The Lord grant that our friendship may be very profitable to us both, and that we may at length meet in that blessed land where parting is unknown.

Wednesday, 12th August

Seven weeks today since we returned from Bridge of Allan, where we were sojourning for over a fortnight. Its lovely scenery and beautiful walks I enjoyed much, my pleasure being greatly enhanced by the company of a friend who is very dear. During our visit there heard Mr Somerville preach one evening in the Tullibody church. A delightful sermon, from these wonderful words, 'Our life is hid with Christ in God'. The discourse was truly elevating and cheering. Two days before we left we made a little trip to Loch Katrine.

The week after our return home was our communion season here, and much valuable truth was imparted. On Thursday, Mr Horace Bonar preached in the morning a sweet and comforting sermon in which the fulness and freeness of the gospel offer were prominently brought forward. In the afternoon he preached an excellent and solemn sermon from, 'I have sinned in that I have betrayed the innocent blood'. In the evening Mr Andrew Bonar gave us a very fine discourse on the Paschal Lamb, as typical of Jesus our passover Who was sacrificed for us. It was full of rich matter, offering nourishment to the hungry soul.

On the Saturday Mr Ferguson, Alyth, preached an able sermon from these words, 'They shall come with weeping'. He enlarged on the godly sorrow those who are travelling towards Zion should know. Mr Andrew Bonar's sermon in the evening was very good indeed. He showed in it very plainly our poverty by nature, and that even after believing in Jesus, we possess nothing in ourselves, but must to the very end draw all our riches from the treasures that are in Christ.

Felt very much exhausted in body on Sabbath night, and was not out on Monday. Although I had great cause to mourn during this season on account of the coldness and deadness of my heart and my wandering thoughts, yet I do trust that by the grace of God it did not pass away without being profitable. Blessed be the Lord that – I think I am not deceiving myself when I say it – I felt at times, in some measure at least, the importance of divine things, and the nearness and sweetness of the presence of Jesus. Oh that my precious Saviour would always continue with me, that He would abide with me forever.

Oh that the oft repeated partings with friends may tend to wean our hearts from this earth, making us feel that we are strangers and pilgrims here, that this is not our rest, and preparing us for that land where parting is unknown. Oh that the Lord would be pleased to pour out upon us the Spirit of grace and supplication, so that when distance lies between us, we may constantly remember one another at the Throne of grace and thus be the means of drawing down blessings on each others' souls. And O make us entirely thine. Bless us with all spiritual blessings in heavenly places. May we be able to comprehend with all saints what is the height and depth and length and breadth, yea to know the love of God in Christ Jesus our Lord.

Heath Park – Monday, 17th May, 1847

It is five weeks today since we came out here for the summer months. The Lord grant they may be pleasantly and profitably spent. May the light of His countenance shine upon our dwelling, and may we be enabled to live to His praise. Many and varied anxieties have of late filled my heart, so that I would not like to live over again such a winter. And yet with how many outward comforts has the Lord crowned us during the past months in Dundee. And I trust I have also been a partaker of that inward and everlasting consolation which He alone can impart. But Oh how many troubled and anxious thoughts have I experienced, some of them known only to myself. And O how disquieted has my spirit often felt, not knowing what to pray for or how to pray. Indeed, the mental anxiety that I have undergone had well nigh crushed my bodily frame, but since we came out here I am better in body and more comfortable in mind. I would seek to wait upon the Lord.

Dundee – 28th November, 1847

Now that we are home again, may the sins of the past summer be forgiven and may our heavenly Father bless us temporally and spiritually, providentially and graciously, and enable us to act in such a way as shall be pleasing in His sight. The Lord be pleased to restore dear Mamma to her wonted health, in kindness long spare both our parents, making them blessings to us, and us comforts to them. And may my brother be taught of Thee and have the peace of Thy children... Eternal thanks for causing him to seek Thy face, and now make him the happy means of leading many to that glorious One Whom he hath found. And, O heavenly Father, I entreat of Thee to lay Thy hands upon us and show us a token for good. Our gracious God be pleased to say to us 'From this day will I bless you...'

**SOME INCIDENTS CONNECTED
WITH THE REVIVAL IN DUNDEE**
During the years 1839 and 1840
By the Rev. Alexander Cumming

Rev. Alexander Cumming was born in Edinburgh on 24th August 1804. He was ordained minister of Dunbarnie Parish, Bridge of Earn in 1834 where by his earnest evangelical preaching he made a deep spiritual impression. He took an active part in the revival of 1839-40 at Perth, Dundee and elsewhere. In 1843 he joined the Free Church of Scotland and ten years later moved to pastor a Free Church in Glasgow. He retired from the ministry in 1874 and died in 1880.

'Glorious things are spoken of thee, O city of God'
Psalm 87:3

Before presenting an interesting case, illustrative of the Lord's work in St Peter's, Dundee, let it be noticed that the sanctuary where the goings of the King were witnessed, was one of the Church Extension fabrics erected in connection with Dr Chalmers' great movement to bring the ordinances of the Gospel within the reach of our neglected and heathen population. Dr Roxburgh, of our Home Mission Committee, was then a minister in Dundee, and entered with great promptitude and energy into this philanthropic enterprise. Through his exertions the church of St Peter's was reared, and immediately, as if to encourage His servants in providing religious accommodation for the lapsed masses, the pillar of fire took possession of it, filling all its recesses with the glory of the Lord. He who has conducted the affairs of our Home Mission with the zeal of an apostle and the tact and sagacity of an accomplished man of business, there earned the reward of his first achievement for the neglected masses, and the blessing which visited St Peter's was a foretaste of the rich showers of the Holy Ghost, which have descended upon the territorial churches over whose interests he has so ably presided.

God sent to St Peter's a pastor according to His own heart in the late Mr McCheyne. During his whole ministry there were droppings from on high, and they increased into a copious flood during his absence in the expedition to the Holy Land in search of God's ancient people. Though separated from his flock, he panted and prayed the more earnestly for the conversion and sanctification of his people. He was, like Moses on the hill, holding up the rod in ceaseless appeal to the Head of the Church in their behalf, while Mr Burns was, like Joshua, toiling in the field of battle, and ministering to his hearers.

At the request of Mr Burns I spent a week in Dundee in November 1839, for the purpose of aiding him during the progress of the revival in St Peter's. The work which God was there carrying forward, resembled, in its main features, that which afterwards signalised the city of Perth; but it did not proceed in so quiet a manner. The cries of those impressed were louder, their convictions more thrilling, and the whole aspect of those assembled in church such as to excite the notice of the surrounding community more strongly than in the case of Perth. The intention of God was perhaps to startle the attention of a large population like Dundee, a thing more difficult to be accomplished than in reference to the smaller number of inhabitants in Perth. It cannot be said that more good was done in Dundee than in Perth; but the convictions of sin were more agitating, their inward darkness and struggles before attaining light were more prolonged, so that the cries and disquietude of arrow-stricken souls drew multitudes from every street and alley of a crowded city of 60,000 inhabitants to St Peter's.

It is certain that those on whom a supernatural change was wrought were not confined to the parish of St Peter's, but belonged to every locality of Dundee, as if it were intended they should be salt impregnating the sinful mass of that manufacturing town, and neutralising the tendencies to moral corruption in every part of it. The work in Perth was like a fertilising river, irrigating the country through which it rolls with a comparatively noiseless current; that of Dundee like a river, not rolling a larger volume of water or enriching a more ample surface, but possessing striking

cataracts and other commanding features of physical interest which attract the notice and visit of travellers.

During the week in November 1839 in which I had the
privilege of being in Dundee, I enjoyed the opportunity of
being daily present in St Peter's Church, of preaching and of
witnessing the private meetings held for conference and
prayer. There were indications of the presence of the Holy
One of Israel, in the awe with which the listening multitudes
were penetrated, in the patience with which they heard the
Word, and the prayerful ardour with which they followed up
the exhortations of the pulpit.

Public worship generally commenced at seven o'clock
each evening, and at half-past seven or near eight o'clock,
when work was suspended at the manufactories, the mills
poured forth great numbers into the church, of whom men
composed a vast and striking proportion. At the close of the
services, on the Monday of the week already mentioned, many
remained behind, tossed with uneasy fears about their eternal condition; and after they were addressed, and most of
them had retired to their homes, about thirty young men,
apparently between twenty and thirty years of age, walked
into the session-house, anxious to be conversed with, and
soliciting more prayer that they might get enlargement from
the captivity of sin.

Mr Burns said to one of them: 'What state do you think
your soul to be in?' He answered: 'I have been looking back
upon my past life, and I see that I have been bound hand and
foot by Satan all my days, doing whatever he pleased.' Another said: 'I see I have not only done many evil things, but
that my whole nature and faculties have been steeped in pollution.' Each of the thirty persons expressed pungent convictions, and then prayer, singing of Psalms, and the

exhibition of the terrors and mercies of the Lord followed till a little after eleven o'clock, when, as appeared afterwards, some really found Christ, and the rest had their impressions much deepened.

One of the most interesting features presented by the congregation in St Peter's was in the number of boys who crowded the pulpit stairs, listening with the most riveted attention, and who remained clinging to their places after the blessing was pronounced, anxious that some word should be addressed to them by the officiating ministers.

Mr Burns, one evening gazing at their countenances, pensive with spiritual concern, said, addressing one of them, 'How long have you been seeking Christ?' and the answer was: 'Two months.' Another, in reply to the same question, said, 'Three months'; another said, 'Four months'. 'But how long has God been seeking you?' it was asked. To this question there was no answer; some rather looked surprised, feeling as if the seeking had been all on their side, and as if God had been carrying on no dealings with them about their salvation.

Mr Burns said: 'How old are you?' One said, 'Thirteen years old'; another, 'Fourteen.' Then it was said: 'God has been seeking you for thirteen or fourteen years, for He has been seeking you all your lives. You wonder He is not instantly answering your prayers, though you have been seeking Him for two or three months; how much more reason has God to wonder that you have paid no attention to His prayers that you would accept of His Son, and be reconciled to Him.'

Then, addressing them in the style of Bunyan in his *Jerusalem Sinner Saved*, he would say, 'I am instructed to tell great transgressors, that salvation is provided for them. When you are convicted as great sinners you may feel like a man summoned into court by the judge – you may say to the crowd between you and him, "Make way for me, the judge has called me". Christ is ordering you to come into His presence; you have a right to press through the crowds and difficulties obstructing your way – through Satan's hosts and all opposition. Dear children, shall we ask Jesus to receive you now?' Oh yes! was the answer – when praise and prayer were offered in the presence of children, not a few of whom underwent a saving change. Some of them are now uttering Hosannahs in glory, while others, shot up to manhood, are fighting the battles of the Saviour in this world below.

I preached every evening during that week in St Peter's. It was not intended that I should officiate on the Wednesday, as Mr Burns, who had been preaching somewhere out of Dundee on the Tuesday, was intending to occupy his own pulpit on that evening. Being anxious to attend the meeting, and having been obliged to go out of town in the afternoon, I made a great effort to get back in time, but could not avoid being a little late. When I entered the church the congregation was singing the psalm subsequent to the first prayer; the elder, who stood at the plate, said to me as I entered, 'Mr Burns feels quite exhausted tonight, and expects you to take his place.' I answered, 'This is impossible without any preparation'; but as I advanced along the passage Mr Burns made signals from the pulpit that I should ascend beside him and speak with him.

With much reluctance I did so. He pressed his request, and said he was so overwhelmed with fatigue as to be unable to discharge his ministerial functions, and that I must labour in his stead. I replied that I was unprepared, but the congregation were now singing the last verse of the psalm. Mr Burns said, 'Stand up and say something in the strength of God, and if you are not supported, sit down.' As he uttered these words, the last line of the Psalm was sung out, and the congregation was hushed in silence and expectation. I stood up and was directed to Zechariah 3, and though nothing occurred which had not previously passed through the mind, it was made evident that when God has immortal souls to feed, He can suggest to any minister, however otherwise incompetent, the suitable topics.

A great solemnity was diffused over the audience than I had yet seen; the stillness became more and more breathless. The speaker, after dilating for more than an hour on the invitations of the Gospel, and the danger of trifling with its provisions, felt impelled to pause for a moment and say, 'Let every person now present follow up what has been said by an immediate dedication of himself to God, who is present by His Spirit, to enable sinners to flee from the wrath to come. I shall wait five minutes that every sinner may flee to the waters of the well of Bethlehem, and break through all opposition in his way.' Mr Burns, who was sitting behind me in the pulpit said, 'Wait, dear brother, till nine o'clock strikes.' It was at that time seven minutes to nine.

I intimated that I would suspend my address till the clock, which was inside the Church, in the front of the gallery opposite the pulpit, should strike nine; and I exhorted the whole audience to deal with God individually, in wrestling importunity, and seek the pardon of their sins and renovation of heart. No one seemed to look back to the clock to ascertain how many minutes it wanted of nine o'clock, but as if there was not time to do this, each person, through the crowded audience, felt the greatest eagerness to find Christ, if not for the first time, yet to get a fresh and more tenacious hold of

Him than ever. Each head was bent down in supplication; the stillness deepened into the greatest intensity, and nothing was heard during the brief pause but the machinery of the clock, or some sob or half-stifled sound of those engaged in supplication. Many prayed as if the destinies of eternity were to take their colour and complexion from the transactions of the evening. The clock sounded after seven minutes of unbroken stillness, and each individual was startled as if the short season had passed without its having been adequately improved.

Mr Burns mentioned afterwards that he had come into contact with fifteen individuals who on that night appeared to have passed from death to life, and no one can tell how many out of a dense auditory, composed of persons residing in Dundee, or belonging to the rural population in its vicinity, may have had a new bias impressed on their character. The impression produced that night, through the power of the Holy Ghost, seemed connected with the persuasion that the audience were not entitled to consider when they would attend to their eternal interests, that God was in Christ ready to reconcile them to Himself, that they were bound to come to an immediate decision as to their accepting the offers of pardon, and that if they quitted the sanctuary without resting on Him as a Saviour, they might go down to eternal despair, as having neglected the great salvation. Many felt that evening they must be saved *then*, or never.

The meetings organised for conference and prayer, which took place after the public exercises were concluded were much blessed to convinced souls, in leading them to peace and rest in Jesus. In the parable of the Sower it is said, Satan, like the birds of the air, watches for the seed that has been sown; and it often happens that, after a sinner is delivered, he stoops down and catches away the seed by leading the worshippers to frivolous or earthly conversation. And it was when hearers carried out the instructions imparted to them by unabated anxiety about their eternal interests, and by assiduous prayer, that the seeds deposited in the soil of the heart germinated and sprung up into eternal life.

Many instances might be furnished of persons on whom the Spirit of God savingly wrought in Dundee. One is subjoined, which signally illustrates the nature of the Revival, and is connected with the wonderful days in the ministry of the late Mr McCheyne. She had been for a long period in great spiritual distress, sometimes on the very verge of despair, when she came to Dundee early in 1840 to enjoy the benefit of the ministry of Mr McCheyne and his fellow-labourers in the work of the Lord.

'Hearing that Mr McCheyne was to preach in Wallacetown Church on Sabbath evening,' she says in a letter written in 1860, and addressed to myself, 'I went to hear him. His subject was "Ye must be born again" (John 3). I felt that I had not undergone this change, but it was my cry to God that His Holy Spirit would work this change within me. I thought I never was more earnest than that night for a blessing on the preached word. Every word that came from the preacher's lips seemed as a pointed arrow to my soul. I prayed that I might be enabled to look to the Lamb of God that my sins might be taken away. I would have liked to speak to the minister that night, but came away without doing so. I could get no rest that night, and rose early to see if I could find out the precious promises he pointed out for us to take home with us. I read much

in my Bible for some days, but had not much understanding of it.

'During that week I again heard Mr McCheyne
preach. His text was in Revelation 14:13: "Blessed are
the dead which die in the Lord". He stood in front of
his own church, and addressed the people in the open
air. He spoke much of the happiness of the people of
God. I was grieved because of my own wicked heart,
and thought surely God was never to save my soul, or
it might have been saved before this. The minister held
up Christ freely to the unconverted present, and then
said, "If there is a soul here today that will perish, you
will remember in eternity how freely Christ was offered to you, and you would not receive Him. I will be
a swift witness against you myself. The very ground
on which you are standing will testify against you. The
very grass which you are pressing to the ground with
your feet will rise up against you in the day of the Lord."

'He saw me very much affected, and, when the sermon was over, he came and spoke to me, and asked
me to go to his house. I went, and he spoke much to
me about my soul. He asked me if I lived in Dundee,
and I told him I had come to live there because I had
heard of the awakenings that had taken place in it. He
asked me where I came from, and if I had ever told my
case to a godly minister. I said I had often conversed
with Mr Millar of Clunie. He pointed out portions of
the Word of God to me that I might read and pray over.
I told him I could take no comfort from the Bible, and
had little understanding of it. He prayed with me, and
told me he would remember me at the throne of grace.
In the course of conversation that night when he saw

my unbelief he said, "Would you be willing to shut that Bible and say farewell to it, and farewell to the House of God, and farewell to the people of God, and farewell to the means of grace?" I said I would not, for I always wished to be in the House of God, where the way of salvation through Christ is preached. And as for saying farewell to the Bible, that was what I could not do, though many a time I was afraid to open it. He asked me to call upon him soon again.

'On my way home I met a godly woman and told her where I had been. She said, "Take care, for Satan will allow you to go and speak to godly ministers and to read the Bible and attend all the means of grace, if you will just remain away from Christ." When I got home I prayed to the Lord for a blessing on the word spoken by Mr McCheyne to my soul. I valued him very much for his faithfulness to me, but I began to fear I was putting too much trust in man. "Cursed be the man that trusteth in man, and maketh flesh his arm" (Jeremiah 17:5) came to my mind, and for some weeks I thought much on these words.

'I was very anxious to get good to my soul by any instrument, yet I never liked to see any one fill Mr McCheyne's pulpit but himself, because he was so faithful in all the duties he was called upon to perform.

'At this time I was very weak and unable to work. I read much in my Bible, and prayed that the Lord would give me His Holy Spirit to enable me to believe His own blessed Word. I went to the weekly prayer meeting in St Peter's, and upon seeing a stranger go up to the pulpit I felt so grieved that I shed tears. The minister, before giving out the Psalm, said, "Is there a soul here that has come to the House of God without having read a portion of God's Word today?" He paused a little, and said, "Is there a soul come within these walls without prayer to God this evening?" Again he paused, and then said, "Is there a soul that came within the walls of the church without thinking that they were going to transact with God for eternity? Well, if there is any soul present in such a case, if the grace of God prevent not, all the means of grace you have ever enjoyed will be as fresh oil pouring upon you in hell!" These words came home with power to my soul, and I was made to see that the fault lay in myself, and not in ministers. I knew that I had not been guilty of what he had mentioned, for I had been reading the Word of God that day, and had often been at a throne of grace, but I was in great fear of dying an unpardoned sinner.' (Here we interrupt her narrative.)

After sermon Mr McCheyne went to the session-house to converse with two or three distressed souls, while I took his place in the church, standing below the precentor's desk. I commenced with prayer, speaking more from the impulse of agonised feelings that throbbed in my own mind, than attempting to frame any petitions suitable to the terror stricken crowd; and in the beginning I said that God might justly take the besom of destruction and sweep over the whole church, driving us all into hell, the destined receptacle of all moral pollution, when, at the words, such rending shrieks arose from many around me, that they shook my whole soul, and made every limb quiver with agitation.

Some who conversed with me next day said their impressions of eternal realities were so vivid that night, that, like Moses, 'they saw Him who is invisible', and that, when these words were pronounced, they felt as if God, so justly incensed at their sins, was about to brandish the besom of destruction, and, treating them as mire that could not be touched with the hand, hurry them by one effort into the pit that engulphs the worldly and impure.

After prayer I proceeded to address them, and present the offers of mercy; and I noticed the writer of the above recorded statements, and among all who stood before me, none had a countenance of such speechless sorrow, and there was none whose body was convulsed with such tremors. I observed an occasional gleam of joy pass over her countenance when any encouraging statements were uttered, but which vanished almost immediately and left her face mantled with a darker gloom.

I said, 'Christ who healed the leper is willing to heal you; He, who was not content with healing the leper, while he bowed at some distance from Him breathing his imploring entreaty for a cure, but who walked up to him and touched his leprous sores, is willing to draw near and touch your polluted souls, and bless you. He knows you are at the bottom of a horrible pit and miry clay, too deep for created eye to see, far less for created might to give aid; but He is willing to reach down his everlasting arm to grasp you while immersed in the mire of the pit, and raise you to the rock, and wash you with the streams which issue from it.'

I observed that the first offers of Christ had the effect that night of enhancing their anguish. Some said afterwards, 'How strange the offer should be so free, while my heart is so hard as to reject it; how strange there should be so much love, and that my cold heart will not embrace it.' The individual I have referred to was supported home being scarcely strong enough to sustain the discoveries of her sinfulness and liability to ruin, which had rushed upon her mind.

In reviewing the transactions of that evening I could not help observing that the minister of St Peter's, whose heart mirrored so brightly the Divine purity, was much aided in portraying the Divine holiness, and, by presenting the beauty of the Divine character, the convictions among his people were deep and solid. But a far greater energy was that night at work than that of man; this I felt, like others, while listening to the preaching of God's servant; and when I succeeded him in addressing the people, and was called upon to stand more directly in the line through which the stream of Divine influence was passing to the congregation, I was convinced that perceptions a little stronger than were then imparted of our nature being defiled throughout, and of lives consisting of an unbroken series of rebellions against God, would make feeble humanity wither and expire.

I remained with Mr McCheyne over the next Sabbath, he lecturing in the forenoon on 1 John 5, while I preached in the afternoon on the scapegoat that carried our sins into the wilderness. I arranged with him on the following week that he would accompany me to Huntly, one of the parishes of the seven suspended ministers of the Strathbogie Presbytery, where I had been appointed to dispense the Lord's Supper, and aid me in that duty, and preach in that parish for a week. He cheerfully complied; he was deeply interested in the contendings of our church, as intimately linked with the prerogatives of its Divine Head. Though God honoured him in planting many a lily in His garden, he was not so wholly engrossed in that work, as to forget that an attempt was made to destroy the spiritual jurisdiction of our church.

We went to Huntly, where his preaching was much blessed. We were both interdicted from preaching in any one of the seven parishes of the Strathbogie Presbytery, and I cannot describe how his bosom laboured with the guilt this country was incurring in permitting its civil courts to encroach on the prerogatives of Christ.

After we had discharged our duties in that place, Mr McCheyne went to Edinburgh to attend the meeting of the Commission, at which many of the ministers and elders of our church signed the solemn engagement in defence of our spiritual liberties; and, although the interesting state of his congregation might seem to demand his immediate attention, he was too well aware of the paramount interests involving the whole Church of Scotland, to postpone them to those of his own flock. And I could not help observing, as, in returning from Strathbogie, I conducted the weekly services on the subsequent Thursday, while he was in Edinburgh, that the blessing was increased rather than diminished in spite of his attention to the affairs of the church.

I preached on Christ washing the disciples' feet; and it seemed to me that I never had seen the crowded audience so melted with the Gospel; they seemed as if yielding themselves to every impression of the divine Word, and as if they could be put in the mould of the Gospel, and receive every stamp it could communicate.

After the blessing was pronounced, I went down from the pulpit and stood under the precentor's desk, when many crowded near me. From the narrative of the individual referred to, it appears that the 130th Psalm was sung, and souls who knew what it was to be in the depths, and to cry out of them, sung it with melodious pathos. I then said, 'Christ is the day's man standing between God and us to lay his hand on the offended God and the offending creatures. After the Fall, the Father, provoked at the sin of man, turned His back on this world, as man had turned his back on God; but when Christ stood in the breach, and as Mediator laid His hand on the Father, He turned round and looked with love on this fallen world. But will you not let Christ put His hand on you? And turn your face towards the face of the Father beaming benignantly on you? God the Father is satisfied with Christ's propitiation, and is smiling on the world for His sake. Are you not satisfied with it? And will you not look towards the Father through Him?'

Some showed great agony pictured on their countenances at this time, from the feeling that they could not go to Christ, however freely the provisions of the covenant were presented, and I exclaimed, 'Say to Christ, Lord I cannot give my heart to Thee, take it, and make me willing in a day of power; I cannot make my heart worthy of Thine acceptance, but take it, defiled as it is, and cleanse it for Thine own service; I cannot enter into the bonds of the covenant, but do Thou stretch forth Thine hand and put me within them.' As these words were uttered, the individual whose narrative is inserted grasped my hand with a strong pressure. I thought it might be some transient feeling or passing excitement; but at that instant, He who said, 'Let there be light, and there was light', flashed light into her soul, and released her from the pangs with which her bosom ached: her long tossed vessel got into the haven, and from much conversation which I had with her at that period, and during the last ten years, and from her holy and consistent walk, I cannot doubt but that this was the time of love, when Jesus passed by and said unto her, 'Live'.

I have omitted the part of her narrative which goes over

these scenes I have depicted, and now give the conclusion of it. She says:

'Before going home, I told the minister what I felt, and that I was now more happy than I had ever been sorrowful, and he bade me sit down and rest myself in Christ. I went home, but felt so happy, and my step was so light, I scarcely felt the street under me. When I got into the house I took my Bible out and turned up to the 103rd Psalm. I cannot describe the joy I felt while reading that Psalm, and this happiness continued with me for a week. After this I began to fear that it was only a temptation of Satan which filled my mind, but I never again had a fear that God would not hear my prayer, nor a fear of coming to read His holy Word after what I felt that night in St Peter's Church. And ever will I praise the Lord for his boundless love and tender mercy towards me in the land of the living, who deserved nothing at His hand, but the reward of all mine iniquities.

'From that time everything wore a new aspect in my view. I thought that the very skies above my head had shared in the same happy frame which I possessed. My mind was so much taken up with spiritual things that I could take no rest at night. I was so happy for a time that I longed to be removed from earth to heaven, to sing the praises of redeeming love. May the Lord give me grace to be ever living in preparation for that great change, and sooner or later, I shall enter into the joy of my Lord, and sing that song of praise which shall never terminate through all eternity. Amen.' (Here her narrative ends.)

I had the opportunity, for days in succession, at this time, as well as on other occasions, of conversing with persons oppressed with a sense of sin. I found, with regard to the two nights to which I have more particularly referred, when many seemed so deeply lacerated with the abasing consciousness of their sinfulness, and vented their inward sorrows in moanings and bitter shrieks, that their impressions did not commence then. 'Their sore had run in the night, and ceased not' for weeks and months, and now the heavings of mental anguish became insupportable. Right conviction terminated in their seeing the sin of their nature, as well as the more prominent deformities which had stained their lives.

Sometimes a recently perpetrated offence stung them with great agony.

A printer's apprentice had sometimes in the evenings, after the hours appointed for labour were over, made use of his master's apparatus secretly to print bills and other papers, and had appropriated the pecuniary gains arising from this to his own purposes; when in the light of eternity he saw the flagrant dishonesty of which he had been guilty, he felt the writhings of the keenest remorse, and was anxious to know whether he should reveal his delinquency to his master, and how he could make reparation for it.

Two young men had, on a Sabbath day, crossed in the ferryboat to Newport in Fife, and had spent part of that holy day in recreation and amusement; and now they stood confounded at their impiety in daring to trifle with the instituted means of grace.

Sins, which at other times many would have thought venial, seemed then to dilate into their real proportions, and to confront them with the recompense of reward that was due.

If the sense of sin was fearful, most of those who got rest

from it made efforts to diffuse the knowledge of Christ's name, and some did so at great personal sacrifices. One young woman, who had accumulated a sufficient sum to purchase what for one in her station was a smart and valuable dress, was so smitten with a sense of the spiritual destitution of the world, as to devote the whole of this money as a contribution to the Jewish Mission.

It is worthy of notice that the rich shower of the Spirit which diffused such precious blessings in Perth, Dundee, and other places in the land, descended in a time of trying perplexity to our church, viz, soon after the adverse decision of the Court of Session in the Auchterarder case was ratified by the House of Lords. The path of duty was plain, but difficult as it was plain, and the copious effusions of God's Spirit told that He was with us.

When Christ constrained his disciples to get into a ship and cross the sea of Galilee, His injunction was clear and unambiguous; a storm overtook them, but this was no reason for turning round the vessel; they rowed against the stream, though making little progress, till their Master came to them, when He found them still steering in the right direction. The path of duty was plain, but a tempest was coming down, and it was well when many elements were lowering against us, that God by the supernatural effusion of His Spirit said, 'I am with you to help you'.